THE MIRACLE CAT

Ceuzinha

ISBN: 978-0-9937058-3-0

Dedication

Dedicated to Leopardo and My Mother!

Leopardo, you came to me as a little kitten and accomplished a huge task. You brought into my life love, hope, and healing.

Mother, you taught me about kindness and generosity toward animals and humans. You, dear mother, were ahead of your time; you cared for animals with all your heart and soul, expecting nothing back. You helped me to see what selflessness is.

ACKNOWLEDGEMENTS

First and foremost, I'd like to appreciate my esteemed readers for the gift of time in allowing me to share my story. May the love of the "Miracle Cat" in your life allow you to deal with your past in order to heal your present.

Special Mention to Lindsay Martin,

A heartfelt sentiment goes to my dearest departed niece, Lindsay. You were a beautiful gift that briefly passed by, leaving an imprint of your precious presence and energy in this world.

Every day as I sign "People's Ethical Treatment of Animals" petitions, your cat, Oliver, cuddles beside me as if he knows that it was you who first told me about this great organization. I love their quote and pray that one day all people will live by it:

"Animals are not ours to experiment on, eat, wear, use for entertainment, or abuse in any other way."

I am grateful to have shared your significant life.

Love,

Aunty Ceuzi

Helga DeSousa

I want to acknowledge you, Helga, for your significant role in my writing of this book.

The first day we met, you shared you had written and published a book. I expressed my dream of writing my story and asked for your assistance. You were my first step in a long, tumultuous road toward seeing my dream come true.

Even greater than donating your time and writing ability, I'm forever grateful for your wise and transforming advice. You also made me realize I could help animals by writing this book.

You encouraged me to share my life as a universal theme for women who have struggled and were shunned for having a voice. This was my opportunity to give voice to my thoughts.

When I considered using a made-up name, you told me to reconsider publishing this book under my own name and assume my identity with pride and not shame. Our love for animals only reinforced a lifetime bond, my "Miracle Cat Sister"!

With heartfelt gratitude,

Ceuzi

Ana Paula Borges-Biscaia

Thank you, Ana Paula, for the priceless assistance you have provided as I faced the closing of this book.

As I turned the last pages of this book, I was confronted by the crossroads of decisions based on the moral content of the revelations in the case and the potential impact on the people involved.

I turned to you as a friend and a member of "let's write a book club," and I found the moral compasses for my decision-making.

Your strong character is built on a foundation of continuous scripture studies and living practice, which gave me the comfort and guidance needed at this crucial time.

I thank you for your willingness to help, your precious support, and your unlimited patience.

Thanks, my "Miracle Cat Sister!"

Ceuzinha

Toni Bianchi

Noteworthy gratitude to you, Toni, for your essential gift—my self-forgiveness. Not only that, but you have also assisted me by enabling me to forgive others and, in this way, helped to restore my freedom. In a way that only you can, you held my hand as you realigned me and made my relationship right with God.

Thanks for being part of my life, spiritual sister!

Ceuzi

Lucia Bellafante

I am grateful to you, Lucia Bellafante, for your coaching assistance.

You offered the right combination of professionalism and personal attention to my medical needs.

You were able to bring out the good from the clouded traumas in my life in a more fair, truthful way, contributing to my healing process.

I learned of your sensitivity to animals, enriching our collaborative work.

I am blessed to have you cross my path and appreciate you as my "Miracle Cat Coach."

With love,

Ceuzinha

ABOUT THE AUTHOR

Maria do Céu Oliveira-Cabral, mostly known as "Ceuzinha," was born in São Miguel, Açores, Portugal, where she lived until she turned 19. In 1976, she immigrated to Canada.

As a widow, Ceuzinha presently lives in Caledon, Ontario, with her son and several cats, along with various adopted squirrels, birds, skunks, and other strays that she feeds regularly as they venture into her backyard.

The author has worked in cleaning services, the food industry, Telecommunications, Air Portugal, social work (employment field as a workforce specialist), and Portuguese language instructor.

While working full time, Ceuzinha enrolled for continuing education at Sheridan College, graduating in Management Studies and Human Resources Specialist. She also graduated in Labor Education, focusing on Human Rights and Women's Rights.

As a volunteer, Ceuzinha raised funds for a senior home, Event Coordinator with Carabram, as a community campaign fundraiser, and is one of the founders of "Amigas" (for more info: www.amigaspioneiras.com). Through "Amigas," Ceuzinha had the initiative of fundraising for medical research in different hospitals and for people's shelters.

Ceuzinha was diagnosed with Parkinson's disease in 2011, but she has not allowed her diagnosis to prevent her from being an active activist.

It is the author's first attempt to write a book; hence Ceuzinha's motivation is to encourage women to share their experiences as victims of abuse. As a sequence to Miracle Cat, the author has begun her second book, "Pets for Parkinson's," and research for her third project. Ceuzinha does not let a day go by without signing pro-animal petitions.

The author's commitment is to continuously grow in God's faith and to be able to assist others in their healing process. Even greater is Ceuzinha's motivation to help animals by using all profits of her book "The Miracle Cat" to set up a shelter where all cats and dogs will be taken care of for the remainder of their life, free of threat, violence, or hunger.

PREFACE

Life is far more interesting when we throw out the rules and approach it from a place of authenticity, creativity, and joy. To honor this, I, Maria do Céu, better known as Ceuzinha, am writing my memoir and beginning the first chapter with an explanation of why I'm writing and sharing my story with the world. First of all, it is all based on truth; there is no embellishment. Everything you will read is the truth, as I remember it. I have realized that it is true when they say, 'truth is stranger than fiction.' As I narrate my story to my scribe, I too can't believe that all of this has happened to me. Sometimes it becomes too heavy, and I need to stop and step back from reality. Sometimes I am in shock as I relive my various traumas. I will now share why I am writing and sharing my story with you.

The main reason I am sharing my story is to use the sadness of the past and somehow convert that 'bad' to good. Nothing can alter the past, but to give value and to give purpose to what seems to have no purpose is my desire. I'm hopeful that my history will somehow validate the experiences of other women. Whether someone has gone through the same experiences as myself or something completely different, I want that person to think and know and feel that there is a purpose and meaning to their suffering. If we can learn from each other's pain, then the pain is somehow lessened.

Secondly, it's my desire that any profits derived from this book will go toward the creation and maintenance of an animal shelter in Portugal, preferably my childhood home will be turned into a shelter because that is where my mother rescued every animal that needed rescue during her lifetime.

It was, after all, a kitten named Leopardo who truly inspired this story. Leopardo came into my life unexpectedly and quite by surprise; his effect on my psyche has long survived his short time with me. We were together for five years. Leopardo passed away needlessly through the careless actions of a veterinarian. I even went to court for what happened to Leopardo and was rewarded $3,500.00. That money paid for a surgery that saved another cat. The big victory was in feeling justified; the victory was that it was acknowledged by the law that my Leopardo died when he didn't need to.

During the first draft of this book, I wrote a scene, a daydream fantasy-like scenario, where I was in an airplane flying to Portugal. In my fantasy, I had won millions, and that meant that as soon as I landed in Portugal, the dream of my animal shelter could become a reality. My shelter would be situated on the land inherited by my mother from her father. At just over nine acres, there would be enough land for all the cats and dogs that needed to find safety and permanent home. Today, that land is being fought over by my two brothers, but in my dream, that land belongs to me and all the animals I will save.

I knew that my mother would be smiling as she watched over me. She would approve of my state-of-the-art veterinary facility so that no animal would be left behind without medical treatment. My mother would approve of the other changes too. There used to be a blue and white ceramic sign in the form of the traditional tile and glazing known as "azulejos" that stood in front of our house that said, "Life is Worthless Without Friends," but in my dream, that sign now reads, "Abrigo Olívia Porta Aberta," meaning "open door," because my mother had an open-door policy for any stray animal that walked by her.

If you visited "*Abrigo Olivia Porta Aberta*," you would see lots of volunteers happily keeping all the cats and dogs entertained and comforted. You would also find a large garden where vegetables are grown both for animal and people's consumption. There would be fruit trees dotting the landscape and refreshing ponds where animals could drink from or swim in. Just like during my mother's lifetime, no leashes nor chains were allowed.

I envision this as a Garden of Eden for animals. I also see it as a sanctuary for myself. Not only would the house where I lived as a child be turned into an information center, veterinary clinic, and state-of-the-art food preparation for all the animals, but it would also be my permanent home. Luckily my childhood home is large enough that everything needed, i.e., office space, storage, and educational material, would all be in one location. What a joy it would be to wake up under the bright Portugal sun and walk out the front door to see all the different varieties of cats and dogs living in a relaxed state. As I imagine this, I can feel the peace and happiness of the animals, and I, too, feel extreme peace and bliss.

I've been told that it's good to keep seeing my dream and visualizing it because it will bring it into reality. I will hold onto that vision of my shelter, my sanctuary until it has materialized. And so, dear reader, we are brought back to the urgency of writing this book and why it is so important to me to write it now, even though it is not an easy task.

I have Parkinson's Disease. In 2011 at 56, I was diagnosed with Parkinson's disease. The irony is that my father was diagnosed with Parkinson's at the same age. I have often wondered about this. I can see a parallel in us; abuse toward his naïveté and kindness versus my multileveled abuse, which I will further itemize.

Parkinson's is a cruel and progressive brain disease that leads to shaking, stiffness, difficulty walking, balance and coordination problems, and living independently. There are five stages to Parkinson's disease.

Stage 1: Individuals who experience mild symptoms generally do not interfere too much with one's daily activities. You are still pretty independent and functional.

Stage 2 means that symptoms worsen. You begin to have tremors, rigidity, and changes in facial expressions.

Stage 3: At this stage, you typically do not experience new symptoms, but the symptoms you do have become more pronounced. Movement is slower, balance worsens, and one is more susceptible to falling due to loss of balance and shakiness.

Stage 4 brings about many significant changes. You now experience great difficulty walking or standing without a walker or assistive device for support. Reactions and muscle movements also slow significantly, and it is typically dangerous for someone to live alone due to safety reasons and the need for assistance with daily living activities.

Stage 5 is the most advanced. By stage five, it is necessary to have around-the-clock assistance. Most persons in this stage require a wheelchair. Stage five also brings with it confusion, delusions, and hallucinations.

I now struggle to write due to severe shaking of my hands, and my voice is so unsteady that dictation software is not an option and so I have had to hire someone to scribe for me since both my hands and voice are not good for me to be able to write my story. Like many other events in my life, Parkinson's disease is slowly taking away my dignity, my strength, and my independence. This has been something that I have faced over and over again. Whether my body was being assaulted in one way or another, my freedoms became lost, or my dignity was stripped away, I have experienced it all. Sadly, all these experiences at the hands of people, strangers, and family alike have let me down since I was a child, but never has an animal been anything but kind and loving to me.

I refuse to give up on my dream of opening an animal shelter and finally living my life free of fear. I have witnessed first-hand how animals love you unconditionally and don't desert or hurt you. I have a great need to give back to the animals since, as I mentioned, it was Leopardo who saved me. You will learn all about

Leopardo when I share exactly how he appeared in my life and how his love unlocked decades of repressed memories.

There is an urgency to get this all written down because I become increasingly forgetful and confused with each passing day. As the pain lasts longer, the periods of rest need to be longer. I must complete this book in enough time to see *my animals* reap the benefits of my tortured life. There needs to be a reason for all the suffering I have endured because what does it all mean without reason and purpose?

I often ask myself these questions: "What does it all mean?" "What is the purpose of all this suffering?" I have no good answer. I only know that I must give my life meaning by sharing my story and thereby giving it purpose. I am the meaning. Saving animals is the purpose.

CONTENTS

CHAPTER 1
My Childhood Paradise

My life had not always been about pain, sorrow, and suffering. There had been a time, although short-lived, when I was happy and carefree. I was born in 1957, 25th of June, the third of three children born at home. After me, the remainder of my five siblings were born in a hospital. We were fortunate enough to live on the subtropical island of São Miguel, Açores, Portugal, on nine acres of ancestral land.

Portugal is the westernmost point of Europe along the west coast of the Iberian Peninsula. Lisbon and Porto are the two major metropolitan areas. If you visit Lisbon today, you will get a great sense of its history since it hasn't changed much since the 18th century. Portugal is one of the oldest nations in the world. Until the 1970s, Angola, Mozambique, and Macau were Portuguese colonies, and in 1999 Macau finally reverted to China. Portugal's strength and power in its colonization were not a reality. I find my existence under the same spell.

I think that colonization is just about power and control. Just as others tried to control and overtake me for their selfish needs, once a country 'colonizes' another country, that country does not belong to the country of power. Many people in my life overtook me, but my soul, my being, still belonged to me, no matter how shattered I was.

Or perhaps I was doomed because eight out of ten Portuguese people are Roman Catholic. In I Corinthians 6:19, St Paul reminds Christians:

"Do you not know that your body is a temple of the Holy Spirit within you, whom you have from God? You are not your own; you were bought with a price. So, glorify God in your body."

Reading those words makes sense to me as to why I never felt like I belonged to myself. But this is now about my happy days, my short-lived happy days.

I loved living in the country, especially since we lived on ancestral land comprising more than nine acres on the island of São Miguel, situated in the middle of the Atlantic Ocean. This meant that the weather was semi-tropical; it was perfect for a child to explore and spend endless hours outside playing with friends. We mainly used our imagination and created our toys and playground. We made our own seesaw out of old tires and a plank of wood.

We were adventurers, impersonating a series of books titled "The adventures of 5," living the different characters with passion and dedication, cooking our fries in a little retro petroleum stove, and making ice-cream in the make-shift playhouse my older brother built from wood remnants. This little person's house was beside an old lilac tree, and the scent was almost overpowering when the lilacs were in bloom.

Lilacs are still one of my favorite plants, and every time they're in bloom, I'm instantly transported to those leisurely days playing with neighborhood friends and eating homemade watermelon popsicles. Watermelon popsicles with no chemicals, no colors, no preservatives, just the natural sweetness of sun-kissed watermelon that was so sweet and refreshing. I have many fond memories of the food of my childhood. Those first ten years of my life were filled with great food, great friends, and great memories. I was free, innocent, and lived in excess. I didn't know at the time how fortunate I was and how much abundance we had as a family.

Mondays and Saturdays were baking days by a lady from the area who would come and bake the bread for my mother. On

Mondays we baked tons of cornbread and Saturdays were for wheat bread baking. I recall my father lovingly saying, "Mondays are for the animals," and he was correct because no one else ate cornbread except for my mother and me. This is important because cornbread was for the less privileged, and we baked it for the animals, confirming our abundance of corn and my mother's sensibility toward animals that looked for her care for survival.

Since Mondays and Saturdays were bread baking days, the oven remained piping hot for the whole day, and we would cook the next couple of meals, including sausages, beans, potatoes seasoned with fresh pork fat, fish, and even dessert on those two days. And, of course, we'd eat lots of warm, fresh bread with butter that melted at the touch of the bread, intensifying the delicious aroma of the fresh bread.

Living on our nine-acre farm was like living in the garden of Eden, except that nothing was forbidden for me. I could pick and eat anything I wanted whenever I wanted. Our farm grew a cornucopia of fruits and vegetables. We had assorted varieties of potatoes, and I remember eating them for six out of seven days. There were string beans, sweet peas, fava beans, tomatoes, lettuce, corn, peppers, onions, garlic, eggs, chickens, goats, and pigs. We even had carrots and cauliflower, two vegetables that were rare for our island, but my mother had somehow procured the seeds from someone on the mainland and managed to nurture those seeds so that they produced a plentiful harvest. These were the only two foods that my mother did not share with others. We had so much kale and cabbage that my mother sold huge portions of kale for a minimal price so that those with little money could afford to keep their dignity while buying the food they needed. Then there were the vineyards where father grew sweet red grapes which he turned into wine and moonshine.

There was plenty to do and eat in the summer, and because our property was so large, it housed a large silo, and this meant that we had plenty of food to eat all winter long, as well as a variety of food.

As you walked out of the kitchen door, you were immediately greeted by a massive cement pad shaded by an enormous grape vine-covered arbor. There sat a water reservoir to the left of our house, which meant we had abundant fresh water. Remember, this was before running water, and we were privileged not to travel to get our water. There was a covered laundry house attached to the water reservoir where the various helpers did all the laundry, relieving the mother of the duty.

Walking down to the right, there was one enormous "Secadouro" that housed the corn for the entire year. To the left of our home was the wine house, or the "adega," as we call it in Portuguese. I was so fascinated by the huge barrels of wine where two types of wine were fermented. In a way, it's fitting that that particular structure has since fallen to the ground, symbolizing my family's fall.

One of my favorite activities was climbing the orange trees, plucking ripe oranges, and eating them right up on the tree. The views from atop the fruit trees were stunning. From there, I could see the fruit orchard encircled by tall trees. Those trees protected the precious yellow lemon trees. There were also trees of plum, pear, apricot, banana, and loquâts—my favorite fruit! Many westerners are not unfamiliar with loquâts; it's a wonderfully sweet fruit that somewhat resembles an apricot growing on a large tree with shiny dark green leaves. This fruit, once ripe, is incredibly sweet; it's like eating summertime. I'd often get in trouble for eating loquâts because they were notorious for staining my clothes.

From my birth until high school, I remember having custom-made clothes. The seamstress would come to the house, take my measurements, and then sew my outfits meticulously to fit me perfectly. Often mother was the designer of those beautiful and elaborate dresses and suits. Mother was a self-taught fashion designer with a creative imagination; her inspiration came from fashion magazines. She had a talent for transforming what she'd seen into something more. Even after having eight children, my mother maintained her elegant sense of style. My Godmother, who had immigrated to the United States, used to send us the most exquisite and colorful fabrics. Silks, brocades, chenille, and organza were the fabrics of my childhood. Imagine, my church attire was considered so special that a more experienced and knowledgeable seamstress came for those outfits, and church clothes garnered two fittings, not one like everyday clothing. I wore a different color dress each Sunday of the month and could go two months before having to repeat an outfit.

As a young girl, I was very fit and pretty. My thick long hair was always worn in two braids. I remember my mother taking great pride and care of my hair, clothing, and looks. I was a regular in the church festivals and processions, often playing the honored part of saints. I believe my mother's promise to the saints, like acts of charity, was to honor them by dressing me up as the represented saint in our yearly village procession.

It wasn't until I was fourteen years of age that I won the battle of cutting my hair, only because I begged and pleaded endlessly, whining about the pain and time it took to wash and comb all that thick hair. It was such a relief once I was able to cut it off. It was a big deal for my mother to allow me to cut my hair because I'm certain that my mother saw my hair as the essence of my beauty.

My mother was a beautiful woman, not only physically, but she also possessed a striking spirit. She wore her thick dark hair in a stylish medium length, and her big brown eyes were always filled with love and kindness. Her kindness extended to animals, strangers, and all those who worked for her. Being part of the few privileged in our town, my mother took piano and French lessons. I share this as a way to illustrate how truly wealthy and privileged my mother was from birth. Yet she was never disrespectful or arrogant toward anyone, nor was she selfish with her time, kindness, or material possessions.

During those summer months, when I spent all day playing

with friends, my mother would call us into the house to eat a lunch that she had lovingly prepared for us. At that time, no one else could do this because money was scarce, so it was a real treat for my friends to eat at my house because we had a variety of foods they lacked. Everything was freshly picked, full of flavor, and in abundance. We had so much that it was a joy sharing with others.

Everyone was of equal value to my mother. Servants and family all shared the same table and ate the same foods simultaneously. There was always a large bowl of fruit on the kitchen table, and once, when one of the maids asked if she could take one, mother replied, “You don’t need to ask. Just take whatever you want”. Regularly my mother gave fruit, bread, and milk to those in need.

Mother had plenty of opportunities to exercise her generosity and did it with great joy; her generosity never impeded our daily needs. I even remember the banana stalks which sat like little soldiers behind our front door, and once, when my curiosity got the best of me, I asked my mother why there were always bananas behind the door.

She told me, "This way, I can give a banana along with bread to the children when they come asking for food."

The midwife, the Saturday and Monday baker at our house, was widowed twice over and lived in a modest, small house that she kept immaculately clean. Mother always took good care of her and ensured that the midwife had milk every day. When the midwife was old and sick, my mother assured me my brother drove her to the doctor for her appointments.

During my childhood, my mother fed animals, specifically dogs and cats, with cornbread and milk, but later she changed it to wild rice, cooked in two big pressure cookers. Mother took in every stray unconditionally and cared for their wounds with a first aid kit. She even dissolved aspirin in milk to alleviate their pain if need be. One small dog, run over by a wagon, survived multiple cuts in his small body under her loving care. My husband named him “Colado,” meaning “glued,” considering his stubborn spirit.

Mother was ahead of her time in respect and compassion because no collars or chains existed for the animals under her care. None of her dogs (I say, 'her dogs' for she was their sole caretaker. Even without adopting them officially) went for behavior training. As an expression of the dogs' appreciation and loyalty, they would daily escort my mother to church, waiting passively at the churchyard, like guards, armed only with love and gratitude. Their behavior was more proof of what my mother used to say very early in my life, "Some food and love, and animals stay loyal for life!"

I also recall my mother making this statement often, "Saint Antão, the animal saint, will grant me the grace of a sudden death without being a burden to anyone, in exchange for nursing his animals."

Her wish was granted when she passed away from an aneurysm on the morning of my birthday. She had no one but her animals to keep her company in her death. Coincidence or not, that is what happened.

One memory of my mother strikes me deeply because it is a memory I blocked from my conscience, not because the memory itself is negative but because I have now realized how true my mother's words were. I was five or six years old and witnessed my mother helping birth kittens. They were tiny, frail, and beautiful, just like my mother's love for animals. As I watched my mother, she said, "Animals are loyal for life, unlike people." That simple phrase spoken so quietly is so ingrained in my soul because I now know it to be true.

I recall a carefree, joyful morning, hopping out of the kitchen in pursuit of my mother and spotting her bending down by the laundry house. I ran toward her to discover that she was helping a cat give birth, which I could not identify with at the time. It was a typical morning on the island, after the previous night's rain where the scent of fresh earth still lingered in the air when I saw mama cat looking for shelter between the laundry house and the volcanic stone wall and my mother reaching out to take the newborn kitten with a twisted paw.

"Praise the Lord!" My mother exclaimed, "Animals, like people, are born with defects, but, unlike humans, they are not ingrates: all you have to give them is some love, something to eat, and they remain loyal forever."

In my child's mind, I could not understand what my mother meant. Still, her words resonated with my soul because some 50 years later, her words rose to my conscience, enabling me to reflect and understand them on personal experience. My experiences now freed words that had been locked up.

She placed the little kitten in the pocket of her duster and told me to get my doll bottle filled with milk, which I did happily, excited to be a part of such a wonderful event! My mother sat on a chair under the vine tree and fed the kitten with my doll bottle.

I vividly recall this loving and respectful occasion wrapped in my mother's kindness and tenderness with bitter-sweet emotions on the reality of her words during my life many times over.

Now that I look back, I realize how sad it was for my mother, in her 30s, to feel that way about humans. I now also realize that to say what she did had to do something with human betrayal.

As I reflect on my life, I sometimes feel like I lived a fantasy and then a nightmare. Life up until the time I went to high school was idyllic. Things had started to change before high school, but I tried to ignore those changes and just focused on the good. I've realized that I've been doing that my whole life. Ignore the bad; insist on seeing only the good.

My father did that as well. Father had a way of ignoring what was happening around him to the point that his denial eventually led to the demise of our family fortune. As was customary in those days, my father didn't spend much time with his children because he was working. The only time we saw father was Sunday after mass during lunch.

My father managed the farm and also endeavored to make a success of numerous other businesses.

At the age of 19, my mother eloped to marry my father. He was the youngest of 11 siblings of a modest family living in Capelas, the next village. Knowing her future husband's financial situation, she appropriated 100,000 escudos (currency at the time) for herself and my father.

Mother and father were lovely and caring people with hearts of gold. Yet, sadly my father was also very naive, and as such, he was often taken advantage of.

I believe one person who hurt my father financially and spiritually was my father's compadre. A compadre in Portuguese is a person not related to you who becomes a special friend because the father became the sponsor of his children for the sacrament of confirmation. This man - this compadre - drove one of my father's trucks, and I believe he cheated my father of much money. There were rumors about how this particular man acquired his wealth in our village. This individual was not wealthy when he first started working for my father, but then as time went on, he amassed enormous wealth but did not do anything to acquire that wealth. He didn't start another business nor buy land; all he did was drive my father's truck. The village snickered behind his back about his gaudiness. He flaunted his ill-gotten wealth by buying wrist watches for each family member. It might seem strange that a family each owning a wristwatch constitutes lavish wealth, but it's true. Back then, no one except the very wealthy had or wore watches. Even during the height of our wealth, no one in my family had a wristwatch.

Eventually, he and his family emigrated to the United States secretly. Typically, everyone knew when someone was planning and working toward leaving Portugal but not this time. Like the thief, he stole away in secret; I suspect it was to avoid any possible confrontation with my father.

The sad part is that my father was well ahead of his time

as a businessman. He was conscious of the need to protect his workers. Remember, during this time in Portugal, there was a dictatorship, and as such, there were no social services for persons who were hurt at work or could not work for any other reason. My father offered each of his employees insurance. Employees were therefore protected if they were hurt on the job since they would still receive payment. My father offered a guaranteed income even when work was impossible, especially in the rainy winter months. I so admire my father's kindness toward all his employees. My father treated all employees fairly and compassionately. Although he only had a grade 3 education, he was intelligent, thoughtful, hardworking, and visionary regarding the rights of his employees. His wonderful attitude and respect for his workers make it even harder for me to know that he was often taken advantage of.

A sad example of the father being taken advantage of was the sale of his village táxi, his most precious possession since it dates back to when he married my mother. This was an emotionally and financially devastating experience for him. The buyer could not resist my father's naive and humble character.

As an adult looking back over my father's actions and his many failed businesses, I speculate that my father had wanted to make something of himself by his own efforts. The land we lived on that enabled us to live a life of luxury belonged to my mother's father.

So really, my father was on borrowed land. His desire to be his own man must have pushed him to start all those businesses. He tried running a grocery store, construction company, moonshine business, and taxi service, and as things got financially difficult, my father had to become the taxi driver himself. All his attempts failed. I was too young to know why, but if I'd guess, I'd say it was because my father was too kind, naive, and unwilling to be confrontational. As friends and business partners stole from him, he habitually looked the other way. Eventually, the stress of all those failures got to my father because my happy memories of a kind and quiet father changed.

He began drinking more and more. As often happens with these things, you don't notice at first because the changes are so gradual until finally, one day, everything is different, and you don't know how it happened. One memory that stands out is when I wrote a letter to my father. I was around 12 or 13, and I begged him to stop drinking in my letter. He did not stop drinking. He never mentioned my letter, nor did my mother, and I have no idea what happened to it.

Much of our way of life changed from when I was born until I was eleven. We used to have live-in maids, seamstresses, and washerwomen. They were gone slowly, one at a time, just like my happiness. Not because my happiness depended on things tied to wealth, but because as I grew older, my innocence and naivety resulted in self-blame accompanied by self-inflicted emotional isolation whenever something terrible happened that I could not explain.

I found my sister to be an enigma. Being four years older than me, my sister was already an independent soul with a desire for all things beautiful by the time I was born. She was strikingly beautiful. Bronze-skinned, thick dark hair, brooding eyes, slim and fit, and always dressed impeccably. She had little time and no desire to take care of her younger sister and would hide away, reading as much as possible. I don't recall much else about my sister because we hardly spent time together.

When my sister started high school, she was eleven, and I was only seven years old. Since our family was still wealthy, my sister could attend high school and live in the city. I remember her living in different homes, but the place that stands out is when she lived in a private boys' boarding house. My sister was granted special permission to live on the premises at the special request of my father. She was very good friends with the priest running the boarding house and also my father's first cousin. She shared a room with the priest's sister, and I can recall visiting her and being impressed by how well organized everything was. Meals were punctual and tasty, prayer time was strictly observed, and the house was immaculate.

Later on, while still attending high school, my sister lived in "Convento da Boa Esperança" -Convent of Good Hope - behind and attached to the church of Saint Christ of Miracles which was only a ten-minute walk from high school. She lived there and was well cared for by the nuns.

The church where my sister was privileged to live was the church that was responsible for the largest religious festival in the whole of the nine islands of the Açores. This celebration resulted from a statue of the bust of Christ washing ashore on the island of São Miguel.

The devotion to the "Senhor Santo Cristo dos Milagres" - Jesus Christ of Miracles - grew into a procession during the great earthquake on April 11, 1700. It stemmed from the incident when the bust fell to the ground during that earthquake, landed upright, and was not harmed in any way. For the first time in 320 years, the procession of Santo Cristo did not take place in 2020 because of the Coronavirus. I share this with you, dear reader, because it felt like my sister was like that beloved bust of Christ, always landing on her feet, never suffering the perils of life and circumstance, unlike myself. High school was not free, and my parents could pay the tuition fees for her to finish seven years of high school, meaning that she received a higher-level education. Directly after high school, my sister went to nursing school. There were few options in the '60s in Portugal for women who wanted a career, and l guess my sister chose what she thought would be easiest for her. Only a few months had passed since the outset of her course when it was announced that a local airline company was hiring.

My sister applied to be a stewardess, was hired, and left nursing school immediately. For a while, she even worked on Santa Maria Island. There was an international airport that served the nine islands. After that, she returned to São Miguel. Her job meant freedom, travel, and fast-paced life. She could remain in the city, living in her apartment very young when most girls and women could not afford that.

There is so much that I don't know and don't understand. My brother, who I looked up to throughout my entire childhood and who had always been my hero, playmate, and overseer, I am deeply saddened to tell you that I could no longer understand his behavior as time went on since it was a total contrast to the true brotherly love I knew as a young girl. His smartness and creativity shined through his passion and aptitude for anything mechanical and electrical. Imagine, for example, driving my father's standard car at the tender age of 10, up and down the "eira" (large yard beside the house, where the yearly crop preparation took place); he impressed me! Another of my brother's brilliant ideas was at Christmas time, I recall. He fashioned a way to have Christmas tree lights light up by taking an old car's battery and somehow connecting the string of lights to it. The same was done to illuminate baby Jesus and I sat for hours in fascination. I remember thinking he was a genius since there was no electricity at the time. I tell you; people would come knocking on the door to marvel at the effect! When I was eight and he was only eleven, he started his mechanical/electrician education in the city, and his absence left me feeling lost and lonely.

With my sister and brother gone, I was now the eldest in the family. There were three more siblings, all boys born before I went to high school. Unlike many other girls during that time, I didn't have to take care of my siblings and act as a little mother because we had many helpers. Remember, my mother had maids and seamstresses, so I had nothing to do but focus on my homework, read, and enjoy the spectacular views from the attic.

There was a small window seat in the attic where you could look out and see the entire expanse of nine acres. It was picture-perfect! The Green Island lay in front of me, part of my village was visible, the mountains were to the left, to the right was the ocean, and far off in the distance was the next village. Every day after school, I'd rush up to the attic and spend hours just looking out the window over 'my paradise.'

CHAPTER 2
The Beginning of Darkness

There is a truth about life; that truth is that nothing stays the same. Things are in a constant state of motion; even when things appear not to be changing, they are. We can see this in nature as we observe the seasons. We see this in the life cycle; we are born, grow, and eventually die and turn to dust. Sometimes change happens slowly, and if it's a change you don't like, you can fool yourself into thinking that things are still the same until it's too late and you have no choice but to admit that paradise is lost. That's what happened to me. The perfect existence I lived as a child began to change, transforming into the hell that would be my life for a very long time.

Hell arrived slowly at first. As I mentioned, my father started drinking more and more. Mother was busy with two more babies just ten months apart. The helpers we had had around the house were all gone except for the cleaning lady who came only once a week, and mother was now responsible for everything else. Even with two more children and no help, my mother remained dedicated to her charity and animal rescue. My calm, joyful existence eroded just as our money and way of life did. Then one day, I had a brilliant thought; I'd escape the craziness of my home life by inviting myself to go and live with my maternal grandmother. So, at 15 years of age, I once again found peace and solace. Being at my grandparents was perfect. I had my room, and no siblings were running around; I didn't have to care for anyone but myself. I had time to read and study, which I loved to do. The only real 'imposition' I felt was the restriction of electricity use; the lights were to be turned off at dusk because electricity was an expensive luxury. Despite being the richest man in the town, my grandfather was very conscious about our electricity use. Electricity was new to the village, and my grandfather would ask me to keep it to minimal use. I had to do all my studying before sunset, and if I needed light after sunset, I would use an oil lamp. My life during my time with my grandparents was tranquil and liberating. Being with my grandparents was wonderful. My grandmother was very kind and took great care of me.

My routine was pretty much set when I was living with my grandparents. I would get up every morning to the cold breeze through the window, carrying sweet chirps of birds on its wings. Then I would dress up for school, have a delicious two-egg breakfast my grandmother used to prepare every morning, and then leave for high school around 7:20. I would wait for the bus that was headed into the city with my cousin, who attended a private college. Since we spent so much time together, she was more of a friend to me than just a cousin. After school, I would come home, and my grandmother would serve me a delicious meal, and then I would spend my time reading and studying in my room. I felt so happy, free, and at peace. It was also lovely to have my uncle and aunt live next door. They were two of the kindest people I have ever known. My aunt was the sister of the village priest. She was also a philanthropist and had solid catholic beliefs. When people did not have medical insurance, my aunt covered her live-in maid's medical expenses. I still remember being so impressed with my aunt's kindness and generosity. My aunt and uncle made a beautiful couple. Along with my cousin, they had an older and a younger son. I was often invited to their wonderful and delicious dinners, where a welcome and pleasant atmosphere reigned.

Then change happened again. I knew that my circumstances

were too good to last, and as it happened with all things good in my life, this period of teenage bliss also ended.

At some point in her life, my grandmother had broken a leg, and she had difficulty walking and taking care of me. I knew I needed to move out because I had started to feel guilty whenever I saw my grandmother on crutches. Even though she never complained about her condition, I started to feel like a burden. Grandma had a broad frame, as big as her heart. Finally, the guilt I felt overwhelmed me, and I went to live with my sister.

My sister was one of the island's first airline stewardesses, meaning she had a high-paying job in the city. My sister lived a luxurious life for a young girl in her early twenties. She was able to live in her very own apartment, buy a nice wardrobe, and travel the world. At that time, I thought this was a perfect life! I started going to cafes, diners, and movies. Life in the city was exciting, stimulating, and freeing. If only I had known what would happen, I would have run from there so quickly and embraced the craziness of my familial home life that I had dreaded before. It was the beginning of my end but also the beginning of my teenage years. I entered my teens in pure innocence. You need to know that at that time in Portugal, there were no sex education classes, parents did not speak openly about sex to their children, and of course, there was no internet. I learned everything I knew about sexuality and female anatomy from an older girl who lived in my isolated village. One day, this *sex educator* sat another girl and me down and explained the facts of life to us. I remember her explanation of menses; she made it sound lovely, but the reality was quite the opposite. Imagine, she told me that I'd have a beautiful flow of rich melted chocolate every month. Imagine how terrifying it was to get blood instead!

Where she got her information from, only God knows, because the explanation she gave me about how babies were born sounded like science fiction. She confidently shared that you would check into a hospital where the doctor would find a vein from the top of your stomach to the bottom of your belly, and then he would cut on that line with a knife and remove the baby. I learned the truth about childbirth when I gave birth to my son at twenty in 1977. I can honestly say that I, by far, had learned nothing to prepare for practical life.

I don't know if anyone could have been prepared for the betrayal I would soon experience. I did not know women's physiology and was unprepared for the outside world. The system I came from kept me in complete darkness and churned me out of the world as ignorant. I'd like to think I was a bright child in my younger years, but none of what I had learned prepared me for this avalanche. Although it appeared as though my sister had a great life, I soon discovered that her life was less than ideal for me. Also, she was sharing her apartment with a man, who, in my opinion, was evil. Not only did he look evil, but he was evil. He would frequently lock away food and whatever else he thought I should not 'touch.' Though I found this very strange, I didn't utter a word because I was afraid of what they might say or do. Whenever my sister was absent for work-related trips, sometimes for three or four days at a time, I was left alone with no money and sometimes not enough food to eat.

Where I had been excited to live with my sister thinking that I'd have a companion, confidant, and mentor, I ended up feeling lost, alone, and frightened. I had no guidance or money to pay for my high school tuition. When I asked my sister about the school fees, she told me to ask my father, and when I asked him, he simply said, "I don't have any. Ask your sister." Since I had no tuition support from either of them, I had to drop out of high school.

When people asked me why I wasn't in school, I'd lie and say that I was going to Canada soon, feeling too embarrassed and ashamed, to tell the truth. I got the idea to say that I was going to Canada from the young man I would first think of as 'My Knight in Shining Armor.'

I now realize that it was at this moment that I started to live a life of partial truths, obfuscating to protect myself. Later on, in life, I understood why people lie - to protect themselves and even others.

CHAPTER 3
Knight in Shining Armor

Not being at school meant that I had a lot of free time on my hands, so I'd regularly go to cafes as something to do just so that I could get out of the apartment. During one of my cafe visits, while sitting at the table with a group of people, a handsome 24-year-old man who had just returned from the military came and sat down with us because he knew my brother. As lunchtime ended, everyone at the table returned to their pre-lunch activities: everyone but the handsome stranger and me. That was the beginning of our courtship.

Since he was waiting for his immigration approval from Canada, he was not working, so he had lots of free time on his hands as I did. Over the next eight months, we spent every day together. We'd have coffee together at different cafes, sit in the park and just talk and watch people go by. He was handsome, charming, and very attentive.

You need to remember, dear reader, that when I met this handsome man, I was sixteen and he was twenty-four. I was naïve and inexperienced with life, especially men. I can recall the moment I fell in love with him; it was when he took my hand and kissed it so gingerly. I felt like Cinderella, beautiful, desired, and special at that moment. I had never felt so wonderful.

This feeling of euphoria lasted for several months. During those first few months, my gentleman friend was a gentleman. He treated me kindly and with respect and showered me with attention. We kept each other company. This was like a breath of fresh air. I finally had someone who loved me for me and who appreciated me for exactly who I was. Then everything shattered. We went to a friend's house together with another couple. Somehow the two of us ended up in a bedroom alone. He locked the door behind him and began to touch me sexually. To say that I was shocked and uncomfortable isn't enough. There I was with my 'angel'; suddenly, he was the devil. I tried feebly to fend off his advances, but his strength and determination outmatched my body and spirit.

I'll spare you, reader, the specific details but know that on that fateful day, not only did my world crash but also did my soul. Even though there was no penetration, I still felt that I was assaulted physically, morally, spiritually, and emotionally. When I spoke up and told him to stop, I was made to feel stupid and weird for not wanting his attention. After finally feeling safe, my world was shattered because I suddenly saw 'my knight in shining armor' as an ordinary lustful man.

I was left feeling confused and as though something was wrong with me. After all, he said that being physical was normal and that all other girls liked to be touched that way. I didn't like it, and it made me uncomfortable, so what was wrong with me? The mind is a wonderful protector. It can hide things from you so that you can go on living life in a somewhat bearable way. That's exactly what my mind did for me; it blocked out this terrible event. It wasn't so difficult to do because he didn't try anything like that again after that one time, and we went back to hanging out. The next disappointment that should have made me realize this person was not the man for me was his refusal to spend my seventeenth birthday with me. I told him how excited I was that we could spend my birthday together, and instead, he mentioned that a girlfriend from the United States was visiting. I questioned him, and he implied that he needed to spend time with her because she was willing to "go further," implying sexual involvement. I know I should have forgotten all about him, but I was lonely. There was no one else in my life. The only affection I received was the affection I got from him, and so I accepted what I should not have accepted, even though I felt deeply sad and hurt.

Soon after my 17th birthday, he left for Canada, and I felt like he had taken a piece of my heart with him. It was easy for me to write to him because I loved writing, not only because it was a form of self-expression and escape but also because it gave me a way of feeling connected to him. So, I took to writing him long letters daily; imagine my desperation! I had to beg my brother for money to buy stamps to mail those letters.

Sometimes I would receive a response, but most of the time, I would not hear back from him for weeks or even months. The most he had written to me was a brief paragraph on a small note. It took many years before I understood that his lack of written communication was twofold; one, he was otherwise disinterested in our long-distance relationship, and two, his reading and writing skills were lacking. My life went on aimlessly for quite a while.

CHAPTER 4
Light in the Darkness

I was alone most of the time. Occasionally I'd hang out with my sister and brother and their friends. On one such occasion, a group of us went to someone's summer house by the beach. Immediately inside, I was greeted by images of extreme pornography displayed on a large screen TV. Feeling incredibly uncomfortable and frightened, I went into another room away from the grotesque images and happened to bump into an old friend. She, too, had left to escape the profanity being displayed.

I'll never forget what she said to me as soon as she saw me, "Whenever your siblings ask you to go out, look for me. You know where I work, and you know where I live. Come to my work at the emergency department or home and stay with me. Do not go out with them."

Whenever things got uneasy or I needed shelter for the night, I'd look for her. I spent many nights sleeping in the emergency room or sharing her single bed in a room she rented and shared with another girl, so I was safe.

Then one day, it was advertised that a course in tourism was being offered for the first time on the island. I immediately saw the potential for future earnings. I thought this course would be my answer to finding my freedom and helping my parents with their financial problems. I knew that I had to take that course. I asked my sister for the money to take the course and promised to pay her back as soon as I received my first cheque. Thankfully, she let me borrow the money. I was now enrolled in the Tourist

Guide Course. I loved being back in school and having a purpose. Knowing that soon I would be independent brought me joy and hope. Finally, the day came when I completed my course. I was the only one offered a full-time job at a travel agency. I felt proud of myself and my work and optimistic for my future.

Not long after I started working, the owner of the agency, a middle-aged man going through his second divorce, started harassing me sexually. He tried to have sex with me. He used to call me into his office and lock the door and invite me to go on business trips with him and have lunch with him. I'd always answer the same way, telling him I couldn't go with him because I had a boyfriend in Canada. He always responded the same way, half laughed and half sneered.

During our agency's bus tours to the popular and beautiful Furnas, he insisted I return to the city with him in his car. As I refused, he continued to insist and kept coming closer and closer to me until I physically pushed him out of the bus. The next day when I showed up for work, I was fired.

I wish I had known then that what had happened was sexual harassment in the workplace. At the time, I blamed myself, my jean skirt, and my body for inviting his attention. I didn't tell anyone I was fired because I felt shame and confusion. I had been so happy and grateful to be working, and now I had nothing again. I didn't know what to do. In my young mind, I thought that giving whatever earnings I had to my mother would somehow make the wrong of being fired 'right'. When I gave my mother the money, she was expecting more. I couldn't bring myself to tell her that I had been fired. I remember feeling saddened by her reaction. My mother, who was so gentle and kind with animals, was yelling and speaking to me harshly. I was shocked by her outburst and deeply hurt.

There were many incidences where I did not find what I expected. I had hoped to have a mentor in my sister, and that dream was repeatedly shattered. I still remember the time she yelled at me in front of one of her friends, implying that I was dirty since I had hidden my dirty underpants in my drawer. I wished the ground would have opened and swallowed me up. I never had sanitary napkins, so instead of using pads, I created my own with rags. Of course, this didn't work well, so I'd bleed onto my clothes. Again, I was embarrassed and ashamed of my own body.

Being young, inexperienced, and not having anyone to confide in, I was left to my own thinking and conclusions. I felt like my body was a curse because I kept encountering men who wanted to exploit it, even though I was a minor.

One such time was when I'd gone to my sister's apartment and found the door locked. I had no key. Did I tell you? Dear reader, even though I was staying at my sister's, she never gave me the key, and I was too scared to ask for one! I was completely reliant on someone else for my safety and comfort. Well, on this particular night, no one was home, and I was locked out. It was getting late. My usual friend, the nurse, was not reachable, so I finally decided to knock at another friend's to stay overnight. I thought that I would be safer there than waiting in the street. I should have stayed in the street. Once everyone was in bed, my friend's father entered my room, got into bed with me, and started touching me. I started screaming, and his wife screamed for him and yelled at me that I should go home to my mother. Thankfully he quickly left and didn't come back. Since I couldn't go home, I curled myself up and fell asleep crying on the pillow.

I truly felt alone in my life. There was no one to turn to, no one to trust. As a child, I used to get proper medical care for my reoccurring bronchitis but now, living with my sister, I had no medical care and no one to help me when I needed it. One time, my sister was away at work for a few days, and I got really sick with bronchitis. I don't know where this angel came from, but this man in his early thirties showed up and brought me food, saying that I needed to eat to get better. This was one of the few times in that time of my life that a person was kind to me without expecting anything in return.

This free kindness did not last long. Unlike my sister, who had twenty to thirty pairs of shoes, I only had one pair of worn shoes, and I would often hear people laughing at me because my shoes were falling apart. I was embarrassed but had no way of buying a new pair of shoes, so one day, I borrowed a pair of my sister's shoes. She caught me and was upset and started yelling at me. At that moment, I felt I was worth less than my old, broken shoes. After my sister had stopped yelling at me, I explained to her that I needed new shoes but couldn't afford to buy any. Sometime later, my sister told me to go to the motel down the street, where I'd meet a man who would give me a pair of new shoes. I thought it was strange, but I figured I was just going to pick up a pair of shoes that my sister had already bought and paid for.

I asked a friend of mine to come with me, so I'd have some company. Once I reached the motel room where the man was, he pointed to all the beautiful shoes on the bed and told me to choose the pair I wanted. As I approached the bed to look at the shoes, he came closer to me, pushed me onto the bed, and tried to get on top of me. At that moment, my friend bolted out of the room, leaving me alone to fend off this sex-crazed man.

Again, just before things could get worse, there was a knock at the door. Frightened that he'd get caught, my assailant thrust me into a closet and locked me in. I spent the entire afternoon in that dark closet, afraid to move, breathe out of fear that he'd return and finish what he had started.

I could hear the constant coming and going of shop owners coming here to this man to purchase shoes for their stores. Eventually, the noise stopped, but it took some time before my brain registered that it was quiet. He and everyone else had left the room. Fortunately, he had unlocked the door before leaving. I eventually turned the doorknob and ran to my freedom. I had no way of knowing that I would be the payment for those shoes. Looking back over the events of my life up until this point, I have noticed that I have had to run from the danger of unwanted sexual attention numerous times. I've tried to make sense of it now and then, but I couldn't. When I was younger, and these attacks happened, I thought I was responsible for them, even though I was unaware of how I got trapped in them. I didn't comprehend it; I only felt a great deal of confusion which caused discomfort within me. Now, as an adult, I know that it was not me. I did not do anything to elicit those unwanted advances. It has taken many years and much work with myself to know that the problem was my assaulters and not me. I now strongly believe that I was a victim of reputation by association.

My first memory of being molested when I was around five or seven was from a man I refer to as "homen do beco" (man in the alley). My mother would send me to bring bread to a family of three siblings who, like many others, were experiencing financial difficulties. Their house, though very modest, was immaculate. I remember being fascinated by the simplicity of their meal, yet it smelled delicious. As the brother came in from a hard day's work in the field, they feasted on baked onions and fresh bread, complimented by a bowl of tea. Their mannerism was as inviting as a warm meal. I was delighted when my mother requested this errand from me.

On my way back home, I would stop by two houses down and greet a very pretty and kind girl who was usually outside hanging clothes to dry. She lived with her widower father. One day when I stopped to say hello but found she was not around, I crossed the gate to look for her. Instead of being greeted by my pretty friend, I was faced with her father, who picked me up, lifted me in the air, and started fondling me. I was terrified, in pain, and screaming when finally, his daughter came in the door and screamed at him, "Leave the little girl alone, leave the little girl alone, dirty old man!" He put me down and I ran home. I was afraid and uncomfortable.

I didn't say anything to my parents because I felt ashamed, yet I did not understand why. I now realize I should have told my mother what happened. I would also encourage parents to question their children's silence, thereby promoting the sharing of untold unpleasant situations. I have realized that the experience of that day was the beginning of my acceptance of circumstances and events that I should not have accepted.

I have often faced finding the right words to express myself. I know that exposing someone underage to pornography is a legal offense. After spending most of my life suppressing these experiences, I wonder if my siblings were also exposed to similar events. Since I never spoke to them about it, I don't know if they knew what was happening at that house before we went there.

Understanding events from the past that are 'wrong' from the perspective of my 'adult' self is very different from understanding my 'child' self. Even the first physical encounter with my "Knight in Shining Armor" was molestation because I was minor and unwilling, while at the time feeling shattered and confused. Today as an adult, I do not condone what had happened, but I realize that my 'knight' did not understand that what he was doing was an illegal and immoral act. To me, he was driven by his sexual nature and his sexual needs. In the early seventies, Portugal was feeling the effects of the sexual revolution from the sixties, and those more adventurous were caught in this so-called freedom.

There are some events that I will never understand. Like when the man tried to rape me when I picked up a pair of shoes. Or when the travel agency owner kept making sexual advances toward me and then fired me when I pushed him off the bus. I now know that what happened was workplace sexual harassment.

Looking back over many events in my life, I've concluded that people in positions of power sometimes use it to sexually overpower those who are subordinate to them. The 'me too' movement has reminded me that I am not alone in suffering at the hands of those with more physical or financial power. I know through my healing that I am not alone, even though I did feel alone in the past.

Imagine a child feeling responsible for a grown man getting into bed with her to have sex. Shame on him. But this chapter is not about laying blame; this chapter is about realizations and empathy. Although, I can't honestly say that I empathize with the men who tried to assault me. My empathy lies more with my parents and those who have suffered the same fate but whom I do not know personally. As I began living as a mother and wife, I understood my parents better. I know that my parents were kind and generous people. I know that my parents loved all of their children. I know that they did the best they could as their circumstances changed. I know that when my mother yelled at me because I did not give her more money, it was because she was frustrated, tired, scared, and in need. I know she was not yelling at me but at life itself for cheating her. I know that when my father did not give me the money to go to school, it was because there was no money and not because of any other reason. I know that my father always tried his best to be a success and to have successful businesses. I knew then that my father was cheated by those he helped and trusted. I know that this is not right. I know that it made me sad, and it still makes me sad to this day to know how much my father was taken advantage of.

I have also realized that neither my mother nor my father knew about any of the terrible things happening to me from the tender age of five or seven. My shame and fear kept me from saying anything to my parents. I've since gained a deeper appreciation that you can't help someone if you are unaware of the situation. How can I blame them when the culture instilled wrongs in society by not facilitating proper and respectful communication between parents and children?

We only see the outside of people. We don't know what's happening on the inside. Just like my parents didn't know what was happening to me, I also realized that I didn't know what was happening to my sister and brother. I don't expect the age difference to be part of the equation, as I experienced betrayal from people much older than me. I again conclude that the culture in which society lives becomes the culprit of everyone's misfortune, including mine.

CHAPTER 5
Stolen

Toward the end of the previous chapter, you must have read that I mentioned rape. Yes, I was raped, a fate I wish for no woman or man. The horrifying details of my rape were lost to me until 2010, when Leopardo, my treasured stray cat, found me. My brain had blocked out the entire event in the guise of self-defense and self-preservation. Whenever the glimmers of that dreaded past event seeped into my consciousness, I would quickly dismiss them, refusing to give in to their lure.

I thought it was the best way to move on with my life, but I was wrong. Over the years, I've learned that one cannot move forward in one's life until you've faced your worst nightmares and come to terms with the hurts of the past, learn your lessons and move on. The healing process begins when you allow yourself to admit that you are in pain. If you keep running away from the wounds festering in the convoluted mass of your brain, you'll never be free of your past.

I am getting ahead of myself. Let's take a few steps back and pause on the day that would forever change my life and me. My sister had gone away on a trip, so I had the place to myself, and for many days, I felt lonely even though our relationship was almost non-existent; we rarely interacted. But just the knowledge of her being around was enough to console that loneliness. On one of those days, I ended up hanging out with my brother, his then-girlfriend, and another male friend. To this day, I can't remember how I got there or whose idea it was to hang out. We arrived at a house; a small bungalow located beside one of the major streets that ran to the town square. We walked into the living room that was spacious enough to house a love seat, two armchairs, and a small table. My brother gestured for me to sit on the love seat, and I complied. I thought he would sit next to me; instead, his friend took the seat beside me.

At first, he did not make me feel uncomfortable like other men. It was a refreshing change since most men up to this point had been disappointingly predictable and predatory. I found my body relaxed and my defenses crumbled after so long. He didn't touch me or try to make any moves on me; he only asked me the typical questions you'd ask someone you've just met and were left alone to chat with. It was a nice change from the usual harassment I faced as a young girl. We talked about ordinary things without any alarm bells going off in my head.

Then, I remember noticing that my brother and his girlfriend were no longer in the room with us. I don't know how it all started–how a normal, casual, and safe experience turned into hell, and everything went up in flames. I do remember the way his demeanor changed suddenly, like a chameleon changing its color. Once I realized that his intentions were nothing good, I tried to run and get out of the room, but the door was locked from the outside.

His piercing eyes gave me a scalding once-over as he sneered, "Your brother locked the door from the outside and told me to entertain you as best as I can."

At his words, a shocking and paralyzing feeling settled in my bones, overwhelming every sinew of my body. Even today, if I allow myself to remember, I can feel that same penetrating, unwavering, inexplicable thunderstruck in my heart.

And then all was dark.

The following morning when I woke up, the house was empty and devoid of life. As the world around me came into focus, I saw a half-empty bottle of moonshine on the coffee table. My body was sore. I knew I had been penetrated. I limped to the washroom and found blood all over my thighs and legs. I cleaned up as best as possible, dressed, and left the house immediately.

I recall walking down the street in a daze while looking down at the cobblestones to ensure I was walking straight. I felt nauseous, light-headed, wobbling on my feet, and was just one push away from breaking down right then and there. To this day, I think my strong inner spirit - one that I inherited from my parents – carried my collapsed body through the overcrowded streets. Everyone around me was going about their usual day, unaware of the horror I had just lived through. I was only half alive and would remain that way until 2010 when my miracle cat entered my life and heart. It was then 1975, and I didn't know how to go on. I walked to my familial home and went straight to the attic, my safe place. I found comfort in the sweetness of a warm bowl of tea and biscuits to soothe the ache in my limbs and my shattered body and warm my ice-cold soul.

It still pains me to admit that the day after my rape, I told no one about it; instead, I holed up in my attic, protected from the outside world, and wrote love letters to my rapist. I later learned that this is called "Stockholm Syndrome".

It might be difficult for you to make sense of my actions, but please understand that it was my way of coping. I did not know much, but I understood that something very big had happened; he had taken what I understood was a very important part of me. Somehow I felt robbed, and the consequences of that would be even greater than I could have ever imagined.

I knew that physical intimacy was only supposed to happen between husband and wife, so I wondered, *"Was that what he intended all along? Did he love me? Does he want to marry me?"* Hope flared in my heart.

"Why didn't he just tell me? He must be very shy and couldn't bring himself to say the words but ***showed*** *that he wanted and loved me."* I gave excuses to justify his heinous crime.

This, my dear reader, was the thinking of my tortured brain; it was the only way I could cope. I didn't know what else to do or think. It was the 1970s under the beautiful blue sky of Portugal when parents did not speak of sex with their children and sex education was taboo. The only thing you were taught as a female was that you must not have sex until you are married; otherwise, you will sin and be worthless. I didn't want to be worthless, so I created a fantasy to cope with the horrors of that unfortunate day. During one of my escapes to the attic, I was staring at the beams on the ceiling, and I saw from the corner of my eye that I had a visitor. This tiny guest was enticed by the aroma of the cookie crumbs on the floor. The small creature hesitated at every little move, ensuring he was not in danger of being noticed. As he detected the crumbs with his almost invisible but highly effective whiskers, I stared, mesmerized. The overwhelming temptation of food and the fear of being discovered was fascinating to observe.

I controlled my breathing to avoid involuntary movement that would trigger the iron bed to produce any noise that could startle the little creature.

This little mouse was fully aware and respectful of his environment in such an instinctive manner that I admired him. Today, transporting myself back, I understand that my fascination, even at the unconscious level, was the realization of an appreciation for this creature's ability to know that he must press forward to survive in his surroundings while moving forward in a cautious, mindful way.

Unlike many humans in my life who took over my body, soul, and spirit without the least regard for me, this little mouse took nothing but left me a little wiser and a lot impressed. A mouse is accused of transporting diseases, although it does so involuntarily, unlike humans, who intentionally cause destruction. That mouse has more integrity than many people I have encountered to date. I have witnessed much hatred, greed, jealousy, selfishness, and the unwillingness to forgive. Yet the most dangerous of all vices is invisible; man's ability to be manipulative, deceitful, and controlling. I didn't see my visitor again, even though I intentionally left crumbs for him to eat. I remember having such reverence for that little mouse, aware of his environment and able to subsist on what I discarded. I didn't see my violator for a while due to my escape into isolation.

During that time, I would fantasize about our reunion and make up romantic scenarios of all kinds. For example, I would imagine him taking me in his arms and kissing me passionately. Most of the time, these scenarios ended with him asking me to marry him and living happily ever after.

One day, I saw him on the street, so I went up to him. I was excited and could barely contain my nerves.

"Hi." I crooked out feebly to get his attention. He looked up at me and said, *"Yes?"*

"Don't you remember me? You were hanging out with my brother, his girlfriend, and me a few weeks ago." I reminded him; already this meeting was nothing like my imagination.

"Yeah. I remember." He agreed nonchalantly, then paused and took a puff in silence.

"So, what?" He fired back, still playing the clueless card.

"We were together in the room!" I thought a hint would help him since he must have been drunk if the half-empty bottle of moonshine was any indicator.

"You were, you know ... my first," I said as I looked him in the eye, trying to drive the message home where it was supposed to go.

His indifference and mockery were enough to make me feel worthless and a joke. He managed to trample my pride and dignity for the second time. Even when my rapist didn't want me, it was enough to convince me that I was at the same place where it all had started - alone and soiled. This time there was no escaping from my reality because my rapist had shattered my fantasy, the only thing keeping me sane. This time there was only me and my shame.

My shame...

I have since learned that it's not uncommon to feel the way I did after being raped. Many block out the traumatizing incidents in hopes of continuing their lives normally. Most don't even get the police involved to keep their mental trauma to a minimum.

I also learned that feeling numb and disgusted with your body is not uncommon. It is common to feel shame, guilt, and responsible for everything wrong with your body. At the time, I failed to make sense of my circumstances and ridiculed myself. I felt disgusted with my own body and found it hard to deal with the overwhelming emotions like shame, fear, guilt, and responsibility. The most damaging feeling was knowing that a part of me was gone and that I could never be whole again. Within my innocence, the trust in the human race was also lost. Worst yet, I had lost touch with my inner self forever!

Along with a part of me disappearing, my mind also froze. Remember when I told you that right after the rape, I started writing love letters to my rapist filled with romantic fantasies and heart-fluttering scenarios? After his revelation, my true ability to write deserted me.

Until that day, I had been an avid writer, and suddenly, I was blank. I couldn't write anything even though my article, "Now Women Use Pants," was chosen and published in the city's newspaper at the age of eleven. I had even authored a play from beginning to end that won first prize at a local festival. But that was all gone after this invasive assault, which depleted me of all my emotional and physical functions, especially my creativity for writing. My soul was naked and exposed, and I felt alone, frightened, ashamed, and guilty. Most of all, I thought that a part of me that I valued – that I cherished - was gone and would never come back.

For over thirty years of my life, I buried my pain and humiliation through denial, work, and self-loathing. Only the miracle of Leopardo's presence managed to unlock my past and give me the strength and courage to face it. Leopardo's unconditional love and acceptance gave me the resolve to acknowledge what had happened all those years ago and move forward in my life. I now understand the saying, "People who are raped are only half alive because a part of them dies forever." At present, I am recovering by facing my past, learning from it, and constructively moving forward by applying what I've learned through the creation of this book to honor a few people in my life and Leopardo's.

Yet, before you and I can move forward together, I must go back in time, for the last time, and share how I ended up in Canada. I will share the story of my struggles as a rape victim who is unconscious of the many cruel ways it affects your decisions, actions, and thinking. I will share how I hid from myself by accepting a life full of pain, sacrifice, and constant work.

CHAPTER 6
New Old Life

How does one move forward from an experience as harrowing as rape? I don't think there will ever be a simple answer to that question. One has to live through it to understand the pain and trauma rape survivors go through, but no one would want to invite a fate like that upon themselves or anyone else. Notice that I have used "survivors" instead of "victims" for those who experience the horror of rape because being able to put it behind you is a remarkable feat. Everyone employs a different method to battle their demons, and I'll admit my method wasn't something a therapist would have recommended, but it was what helped me survive, albeit inefficiently.

I pushed it deep within my subconscious until I temporarily forgot that it had happened, but the scars persisted. I now realize that doing so meant that most of my decisions from that moment forward were determined by a deep, unconscious, and conscious thought of worthlessness. My life was of little value to me, and I assumed I was disposable. I believe that my undisputed acceptance of all things terrible in my life resulted from being raped. When part of you is gone, taken savagely, and you are left feeling less than whole and alone, you think and do things that are not in your best interest; that was me. I lived to exist for most of my life after my early teens and until Leopardo entered my life. The sadness, resignation, and confusion burrowed deep within my mind were what brought me to Canada. As I entered the house, I overheard my mother on the phone telling someone that I could not go for my interview with the airlines because I was getting married and moving to Canada. There was no mistaking the joy and pride in my mother's voice, and I felt a decision had been reached in my absence regarding where my life was headed. At nineteen, I was burdened by my mother's expectations but what I needed was a shoulder to cry on about my untold secrets. From my late teens to fifty-three years old, I lived in a fog and on autopilot, with most of the details of my life being absorbed by grief and self-loathing.

Let's spring forward to my life in Canada.

Before ever arriving in Canada, I arrived in Fall River, Massachusetts, United States, because my sister could get me a free airline ticket to Boston. There, I stayed with my Godmother for two weeks; they were by far the best weeks of that journey. My Godmother treated me well, ate heartily, rested in comfort, visited my cousins, and went sightseeing with them. Although living with her was pleasant, I was nervous because I didn't know how to get to Canada, and my future husband didn't say anything about picking me up when I called him.

Two weeks after arriving in Massachusetts, I decided to set off for Canada. I could speak a little English because I studied it for three years in high school. There was no plan, or route, just me, my wits, and the desperate need to feel settled. I grabbed my little suitcase and left Massachusetts with the little change I had left from the $140 I had initially brought from Portugal.

Not knowing where to go or having a map that outlined my route, I repeatedly got onto the wrong bus and became dependent on the kindness of strangers to guide me in the right direction. I remember how those helpful people would look at me with intrigue, surprise, and worry whenever I approached them, lost and scared. I'd tell them that I needed to board the bus heading to Toronto, Canada, and they'd give me directions and help me however they could.

Somehow, I arrived at the bus terminal in Toronto, where a

strange man called my name; he turned out to be my future husband's brother-in-law. At that time, my future husband worked two daily full-time and evening part-time jobs, justifying his absence on my arrival. I was nineteen years old, feeling scared, lonely, and disappointed that a stranger had come to collect me.

Even though I lived with my soon-to-be husband, his sister, her husband, their one child, my soon-to-be mother-in-law, her mother, and my then seven-year-old future sister-in-law, I felt alone and lonely. I recall a warm surprise greeting from a beautiful, smiling, sky blue-eyed girl who awaited my exit from the washroom to pay me a compliment, saying, "Tu es bonita!" which means, "You are so pretty!" To this day, she remains not only part of my family but also a good friend. Her words meant so much to me as I was feeling downtrodden.

I felt like a stranger in a house full of people and was receding into my shell. To be honest, I was a stranger to them as well. I'm certain that I was not what they had been expecting. Here was a young girl dressed simply with only one small suitcase. Back home, the perception was that if your family possessed the land, you would be wealthy and equipped with a dowry. This was not the case; in their eyes, I was just a simple girl.

"I can't sleep. Let's go for a drive." He suggested, and I knew he was expecting me to comply.

I was his soon-to-be-wife and lived in his sister's house, so I had no other choice.

"Okay, but I need to change," I told him, and he nodded in acknowledgment.

I can't quite recall my feelings when he asked me to join him except for confusion and a lingering hesitancy. Despite my reservations, I closed the door and flicked on the lights to change into my day clothes. We sneaked out of the house together and gently locked the door behind us so as not to wake anyone. During the drive, it felt like the days when we chatted in the café and walked through parks warm and familiarly.

"Maybe this is love?!" I remember wondering while seeing the world outside move past in a blur.

He pulled the car into a park and drove over to the riverbank's edge. He turned off the ignition and turned in his seat to look at me. He had this longing in his eyes that I had seen in men before. He was going to be my husband, so I knew it had to be different with him.

"I shouldn't resist and just let it happen," I thought as the intensity in his gaze singed my skin. I was hoping it would not be something like I had seen in the pornography movie back in the summer house in São Miguel. He reached in for me, and I felt that I had no power to resist or reject my husband-to-be, so I let myself drown in the sensations evoked by his touch. When he was finished, he immediately removed himself from me as if revolted by me. I watched him compose himself, yet nothing could prepare me for what happened next; he slapped me hard across the face–I felt the burn of that slap on my face for the rest of my life. Instinctively, I covered my face with my hand and turned away from him. I had nothing to say in my defense because I knew he wouldn't believe me. We drove home in silence, but my mind buzzed with thoughts and questions.

To this day, I can still feel that slap and the sting of his reaction both on my face and soul. I never dared to tell him what had happened to me, nor did I have the courage to confront him about his reaction to my not being a virgin. Speaking about it felt and still somewhat does feel like I was returning to that horrific day. I insisted that it remain in the past and in my subconscious mind.

"Is he still going to marry me?" was the question that haunted me every day until the day we got married at city hall.

His sister pre-arranged this because I needed to apply for landed immigrant status since I was only a visitor in Canada. Soon after, I suspected I was pregnant.

A few months later, we had a church wedding with a reception. My dress was lovingly hand-made by my husband's aunt, a talented seamstress; I'm so grateful for her generous gift. To this day, I love that dress. I drew the design for it myself, and I am particularly fond of the delicate white flowers and bright yellow roses his aunt sewed meticulously onto my dress. Although there were over one hundred people at that reception, the only people I knew were my aunt, my cousins, and a few friends from high school. My parents were not present, and I didn't even register their absence because I was detaching myself from that old life and grasping the roots of the new one.

While exchanging the wedding rings, they both fell on the floor. Those two rings were made, in São Miguel, from broken pieces of gold gifted to me by my grandmother. Ironically, the falling of these rings symbolizes my fallen past and unbeknownst future. As a side note, many years later, I heard over the grapevine that I had stolen that gold from my family when, in actuality, that gold had been given to me by my grandmother as a gift.

To my surprise, after the reception, he drove back to his sister's house when I commented, "I don't think we're supposed to come here...we're supposed to go somewhere else." With no comment, he drove away, and I faced this disreputable motel surrounded by strip clubs for our wedding night, leading me to believe that this was what I deserved. I was dismayed by the realization that our wedding night was not important enough for planning.

Arriving at the room, I locked myself in the washroom, turning on the tub water with full strength to drown out the sound of my crying. I felt that he had chosen that motel on purpose; it was his statement regarding the dignity and character of his wife. Again, I felt that it was settled right there and then that I would pay for my *sins* for the rest of my life with him. I composed myself and opened the bathroom door reluctantly, clutching the sides of my clothes in fear. I had my suspicions about the outcome of my wedding night when I saw my husband sound asleep on the bed. This was the ramification of an open bar at the reception, which brought me great relief. I was overwhelmed by God's grace and was grateful for His kindness. I slipped into bed beside my husband and fell asleep immediately, exhausted by pain.

I received my work permit almost immediately and started working as an office cleaner, introduced to me by my sister-in-law, who supervised a cleaning company. My tenure was seven months into pregnancy. I was grateful to have a job so that I could contribute to our income and was spared from the hassle of transportation since my sister-in-law drove.

A few months after being married, we, along with his sister, went looking for our own place to live. I was shocked by the places we were looking at; they were tiny, run-down, and depressing. The reality of being an immigrant was hitting me hard – up until now, my knowledge of foreign lands came from the black and white movies I had seen in Portugal. I had a different illusion of what Canada and the U.S.A. looked like - big and beautiful homes with handsomely dressed people going to parties and eating in fancy restaurants. Instead, the most affordable accommodations induced long regretful cries into my pillow to suffocate the loud sobbing of yet another nightmare. I only saw my husband late at night when our only form of communication was through physical intimacy.

We soon moved out to a tiny flat. Back in the '70s, people transformed the upper part of their homes into rental accommodations. A two-bedroom space became the kitchen, living area, bathroom, and bedroom. It was so cramped that every time we wanted to open the fridge door, we had to move one of the chairs of the two-person table out of the way.

I spent the duration of most of my pregnancy hungry, overworked, afraid, lonely, and ashamed. I recall the day when in the final month of my third trimester, in early July, I opened the fridge to cool myself – my only form of air conditioning - and I saw two eggs. I was so excited, thinking that I had food for two whole days, one egg per day. When I think back on that, I don't know what was sadder, the fact that I only had two eggs or the fact that I was happy about having two eggs, which to me sadly confirms acceptance of my situation. Ironically, as a teen, when I lived with my grandmother, she would cook me two eggs every morning for breakfast.

Money was so scarce that once, all I had to eat was a handful of cereal with water. As I was eating, I felt something crunchy in my mouth; I knew what it was, but I couldn't afford to spit out the cockroach along with the cereal because it was the last of the cereal. When I finally reached out to a family member and let them know I had no food nor money to buy food, I was told that they did not have money to give me but that I could go over to eat on weekends. As if a pregnant woman could wait for weekends only to feed herself and her unborn child.

Soon after the move and before our son's birth, my husband was laid off from his full and part-time jobs. To this day, I can't remember exactly what happened; all I remember is that he stopped going to work and began spending all his time in cafes and bars. He spent his days drinking away the little money we had. I was always hungry, tired, and lonely, yet he was indifferent to our well-being. The kind of desperation I felt during that time was immeasurable.

This desperation continued even after our son was born. I recall times I'd get on my knees to scrounge for loose change fallen from his pants, just so that I could buy the 99-cent baby formula.

One day, from my tiny flat window, I spied some turnips in the landlord's garden and got excited. I figured that if I could get some turnip leaves, I would make a delicious soup, even though potatoes were only an aspired dream. There were times when I couldn't feed my baby anything other than cabbage water; it gave my poor baby such terrible gas that I felt sad and guilty. The cabbage water was my last resort when I couldn't rustle up the 99 cents for the formula milk. At night I'd cry, stifling tears into my pillow from fear of being heard by the landlord.

Again, I created the illusion that if we were to save money and have our own house, everything would work out fine. I remember my childhood basic needs – food, shelter, clothes - being abundantly met, complimented by joy and peace. After living in such a spacious home as a child, I became imprisoned by a lack of family, a depressing environment, shame, and ignorance. In comparison with my old life in Portugal as a young child, I was now in another new hell. My childhood was heaven, and now the baggage of my shame, regret, fear, and poverty was hounding me into this new life so that my new life was not really new but a bastardized version of my subconscious denial.

Despite all my trauma and hardships, one thing that had not changed was how naive I was. Even though I was pregnant, I didn't know what to expect. Not only did I not know how to properly care for the two of us but had I known, I wouldn’t have had the means to care for us. I always say that my son was born hungry because I was hungry for love, food, rest, and respect while I was pregnant.

A perfect example of the chaos in my life was on my 20th birthday. Both my father-in-law and husband were quite intoxicated, which probably explains the family turbulence of that day at my sister-in-law’s house. When it was time to return home, we gave a ride to two other family members. In the name of insensitive fun, my husband drove erratically – swerving all over the road, accelerating, and abruptly applying the brakes. When we dropped them off, one told my husband, “You don’t have the conscience or the respect for your wife’s condition.” Unfortunately, this remark did not change the way my husband continued to drive. I recall feeling my shrunken, frightened fetus seeking protection. I held on to the dashboard of the car, feeling terrified. After that birthday, I didn't celebrate another one until I was in my sixties. It was Leopardo’s unconditional love that helped me soothe the terrible birthdays from 17 onward. I realized that I would intentionally work late every year on my birthday to rein in my expectations. It was the only way to make sure that I wasn't disappointed at the lack of effort from my husband because nothing good ever happened on my birthday. Keeping my expectations low was instrumental to keeping myself emotionally stable.

There were times when my husband would drop me off at his mother's, eat and then go out. To add insult to injury, one time, a family member caught me eating his leftovers and started laughing hysterically, causing me embarrassment and humiliation. That wasn't the only kind of embarrassment I was subjected to – my father-in-law once bragged about his son's boasting of fooling around with women and insinuating that I was none the wiser. I still remember exactly how I felt at that moment - shocked and disgusted. I couldn't then and cannot now understand why he would feel joy in passing on this information to his daughter-in-law, who was pregnant with his grandchild.

I now understand the chain-like order of behavioral events that appear to have negatively affected my husband and me. My husband's father lacked the constructive character to pass on to his son, and I, consequently, suffered the ramifications of it along with my son. Having this as an example, I believe it's a big missing link in society at large. To everyone's detriment, we all indirectly suffer from persons who lack character. The night I went into labor, I didn't realize it was happening; all I knew was that I was in excruciating pain. I got out of bed so as not to wake up my husband and sat in the living room. I held onto my baby, rocking myself back and forth all night long until, finally, in the early morning, my water broke. I forced my husband to get out of bed and drive me to the hospital as I reached for the shopping bag containing two pieces of baby clothing, which cost me $2; this made up the whole trousseau. The drive to the hospital was brutal and terrifying. We arrived at the hospital at 8:06 a.m., and my son was born at 8:26 a.m.

The day my son was born, there was a terrible thunderstorm and a power outage. Because of this, I had no visitors on the first day, but then my husband and a couple of family members came to visit on the second day. None of them, including my husband, brought anything for the baby or me; they seemed to be there to fulfill an obligation. I was sad and disappointed because the other women around me were getting flowers and gifts. Although I was happy for them, I felt like a second-class person yet again. In the hospital, happiness and joy were all around me, except that none of that happiness or joy reached my baby or me.

I remember feeling so sad and disappointed that I wasn't even given a baby shower, not because I wanted luxuries or wanted to be fussed over but because I needed the necessities for my infant child. This lack once again reinforced everything that was wrong in my life. Luckily, back then, after having a baby, you were able to be in the hospital for four days.

While in the hospital, I felt pampered by love and attention, derived not only from the birth of my son but also from the attentiveness dedicated to me from the hospital staff - those were some of the best four days of my life in a long time!

I guess I should not have expected anything to change, but for all reasons, I was hopeful. I was hopeful in those early days that somehow there would be compassion, if not love, within my husband's soul. I was wrong! His indifference remained consistent and my hopefulness was crushed. He continued in his old ways - frequenting cafés and bars. The moment I came home from the hospital, I began looking for a job. When my son was merely two weeks old, I had to leave my infant with a babysitter and go to work because we had no food and no money.

Thankfully, I got a job in a French bakery due to my good command of the French language - a glimmer of hope. I was gone for 11 hours a day. There I had plenty of tasty food to eat, such as croissants, quiche Lorraine and savory pastry. It took me three bus transfers to get to work, and every night I'd get back home late. The babysitter would yell and threaten to quit. More often than not, I was saved by a baguette because every day, the owner of the bakery would give me one to take home, and I'd, in turn, give it to the babysitter to calm her down. I never thought I would place such a high value on a baguette! From my meager income of

$110 per week, I had to cover rent, which was $150.00 per month, $30.00 per week for the babysitter, food, transportation costs, and bank loan payment. I struggled to pay rent and was late every month.

During this time, I felt as though God had deserted me, but then there were times when I felt His grace. I was fortunate to have kind and patient landlords. When my son was born, they gifted me a beautiful umbrella stroller. Even in those days, a stroller was an expensive gift. Had it not been for these generous landlords, I could not have afforded to buy such an item. Their gift provided my son and me with joy and freedom to go out comfortably. I did have an aunt here in Toronto who was a very kind and wonderful woman, but, honestly, it never occurred to me to ask her for help.

I think – I *think* because I'm reflecting on my actions as the person I am today and not the frightened, hungry, and lonely young woman I was then – that the reason why I didn't reach out to my aunt was that my pride got in the way. She knew how I had lived as a child, and to admit to her that I was now married but alone, working but starving would have been an embarrassing moment. The most I could do to help my dire situation was to pretend to forget to take diapers when visiting others.

It worked most of the time as people empathized with the situation. Imagine a new and loving mother forgetting her beautiful baby's diapers! Of course, I would have never forgotten them; I just pretended to do so because I did not have the money to buy them. I was reminded by a few people of being absent-minded. That's how my life in Canada started; a life filled with emptiness and want. I had arrived in the country young and innocent, anticipating an incredible adventure with the young and handsome man I had fallen in love with in Portugal. But upon reaching the land of dreams, I realized that nothing was how I had hoped it would be. My life was turned upside down, and within two years, I'd become a wife, a mother, and a desperate woman.

We were able to buy our first tiny home in 1979, two years

after my son was born. Luckily, we were able to borrow for the down payment. As a result, we had a big mortgage, yet we thought everything would eventually get better for us because my husband had gotten a new job in the steel industry through my connection with an old friend from Portugal. For the first time in a long time, we ate well thanks to the generosity of my brother-in-law, who was able to buy food from where he worked at a discounted price. Because of him, we enjoyed an abundance and variety of food. God bless him for being kind enough.

In all fairness, I feel that I must share the lighter side or the gentler side of the people in my life at that time. I have learned that there are always two sides to something or someone, like two sides to a coin. My father-in-law was mentally ill, but I didn't know it at the time. He separated from his wife a few times, and when he was there, he was terribly abusive and not a pleasant person to be around.

To give you an example of how cruel he was, my husband once told me that his father hit him over the head with a hammer. Of course, not having experienced anything like this myself, at the time, I thought my husband was telling me a terrible joke. It wasn't until many years later that I actually figured out he was telling me the truth. As far as I recall, my in-laws worked very little. They had discovered welfare, and that had been their ticket to financial freedom and final separation.

Later in my life, while reflecting on my past, I realized that my father-in-law must have been more tortured than I was at times. I don't think he could cope with the fact that he had to work as a general laborer to make a living and couldn't be the known sculpture artist he was at heart and had been in São Miguel.

My father-in-law lived alone for the last ten years of his life. He was discovered dead on the floor in his small apartment days after he passed away.

Knowing the family relationship dynamics, I stepped forward to arrange his funeral because I believe the dead should be properly buried. I saw this act of kindness on my part as doing a good deed and placing me in a better position in the afterlife.

The unfortunate part is that my father-in-law was actually a creative genius; being illiterate, he created his own way of measuring. When he lived in Portugal, he was a sculptor, and like most artists at the beginning of their careers, his work was unique, and he did not get paid much for his skills, making it hard for him to afford a good living by doing what he loved. In later years when we (the three of us) went back to São Miguel, my brother arranged a surprise tour to view my father-in-law's sculptures in such locations as government buildings, palaces, cemeteries, churches, and many notable homes and gardens. I was pleased to witness my brother's good gesture in elevating my father-in-law's memory.

Let's move on to my mother-in-law - what can I say about her? The truth is that she was absolutely charming and gracious, just like her son, my husband. She had a keen eye for the finer things in life, and like my husband, the two of them were impeccably dressed and always styled. Her talent for design and fashion was afforded by credit. For her and my husband, the idea of credit meant affordability. They were both so fascinated by the thought that you could buy whatever you needed on credit that the reality of having to pay it back did not enter their consciousness. For them, it was important to express their creative nature, and credit made all that possible.

I acknowledged my mother-in-law's form of apology even though I was unable to verbalize it when she said to me, "I know you suffered a great deal, but I couldn't give you more because I didn't have enough for me."

On June 25, 2010, my mother passed away. It was also the day I was born and the day Leopardo came into my life. I believe Leopardo's first home was in an abandoned barn near my present property. He came in the spring to his second home, underneath an unused car parked in the driveway; he came and went between spring and fall. After my mother's passing and prior to my surgery in the fall, my son found Leopardo as a kitten, hiding under the car. To coax him out of his hiding place, my son would leave tins of tuna and water out by the car tire. Leopardo would peer his head out just enough to eat and drink and then run back to the center of the car. Finally, one day, Leopardo came all the way out from under the vehicle and allowed my son to pet him. I remember being worried because my son was allergic to cats, but when he was finally able to pick Leopardo up and bring him into the house, I was surprised.

"What about your allergy? We can't keep him in the house; you'll be sick." I told him worriedly.

"No. I'm not allergic anymore; I haven't had any reactions to Leopardo. Can you believe it?"

And just like that, Leopardo became our cat.

I have often thought about this coincidence and whether it meant anything or not. There are moments when I feel that somehow my mother sent Leopardo to finally heal the wounds of my past. Wounds that ran so deep that I was unaware of how much they had affected me. I had spent most of my life just living on autopilot and soaking up shame and fear. The burn of those wounds never came into full focus until Leopardo's loving presence. I hid from myself and suppressed the traumatic events to the point of losing a sense of them.

I believed in God, and yet God had forsaken me so many times that I felt as though I'd been spinning in circles; the thought alone made me dizzy, leaving everything around me in a blur and making it difficult for me to stand.

Now, I ask myself, "How is it possible for me to end up like this? A cold-hearted woman at age 55 feeling like I was 95."

I didn't have the strength or the courage to face my past; hence I lived a half-life, feeling the presence of an uncanny void within me and always knowing that something was missing and wrong in my life. I lived my life on the edge, fearing that at any moment something terrible was about to happen, and so I was always on the alert, being and acting defensively. I've never felt close to anyone to be able to enjoy the few joys that somehow escaped into my life. I know my mother somehow sent Leopardo to me to heal my heart and help me better embrace the experiences of my life, allowing me to finally let go of that nagging feeling I'd lived with ever since a teenager.

Have you ever had that feeling that something is wrong, but you just don't know what's wrong? That was how I felt every day for the better half of my life. It was only when Leopardo came into my life that I finally realized what was wrong - my heart. My heart was a stone. Leopardo helped me to see that I've lived my life with as little emotion as possible. I did what I had to do; I met my obligations and my responsibilities. I loved my son and always protected him as best as I could, but even with him, I could never really love him the way I wanted to because that would mean opening up and bearing more pain than I could endure.

When I first let myself remember and feel, I had to admit to failure. I failed myself and my son but not intentionally; I always tried my best and did what I could to move our life forward. Until Leopardo's presence, I did not realize I had to admit to the memories of the past that were locked inside me in order to let go of all the pain that lived in my heart. Remember when I mentioned that Leopardo came into my life at the time my mother passed away? Leopardo first came into my life at that time, but that's not when he became a part of the family full-time. It was later that year that Leopardo came into my life permanently. His timing was perfect because had he stayed earlier, I don't know if I would have been able to hear his lesson.

During the four months, while I was convalescing at home from my surgery, this little kitten did not leave my side. Every time I got up, he'd get up and follow me. Leopardo not only physically followed me around the house but also kept watch from afar. For example, if I were moving my hands while sitting down, he'd watch every movement. Moreover, whenever I was seated or in bed, he'd curl up on my lap.

It was in one of those times when Leopardo was curled up on my lap and gently purring that I felt the intensity of the moment, and the miracle happened! For 45 years, I've lived in fear, denial, and despair. Leopardo was warm and soft, wanting nothing from me except my love and authenticity, which had never been enough for others. However, loving Leopardo and enjoying his company was enough to warm my heart and soften it. I literally felt the stiffness in my heart and body melt. I parallel it to a fast ice melt after a harsh winter. I felt relief as I welcomed the first memory to surface in my conscience.

CHAPTER 7
Awakening and Thankfulness

In this last chapter, I hope to share my awakening...

In spite of all the abuse, neglect, and sadness, I look back and see it all from a different perspective. As I mentioned numerous times, it was Leopardo that helped me come to this awakening. That little kitten was the beginning of my freedom from a past filled with pain and regret. It was Leopardo who helped me find the strength to review my life and forgive myself and all those persons in my life who have caused me pain. Leopardo helped me to find the strength to face many truths. I stayed with my husband for 14 years, and then finally, after multiple moves, personal disappointments, and an exhausted spirit, I'd had enough. I separated from my husband. There was so much upheaval in my life even though I constantly worked and focused on the future, it felt as though I'd take a step forward and then three back.

Always thinking practically, I remember buying our first house in 1979. I was desperate to get our own decent house and leave the third flat in Toronto, so one day when I saw an advertisement in the newspaper for a new builder promoting new houses in Brampton (about an hour North of Toronto), I pointed at the paper and said, "We are buying this house! We have one year to get the needed down payment."

"If we do not buy a house and get a decent place to live, I'm moving with my boy back to Portugal; even if I have to live in my father's wine house, it will be better than this."

That assertive position was a good thing. We bought the least expensive house that the builder offered. Six years later, we ended up buying the house that my sister-in-law had originally purchased. While I purchased the most economical house, she had purchased the most expensive house, and now I was moving into it. I was moving up in the world! I felt proud and had a great sense of accomplishment.

I want to take a detour for a minute and speak about my sister-in-law. She was my neighbor and surrogate sister because she was 10 years older than me. Since we all worked shifts, there was always a family member to take care of my son and his two cousins - that was a great relief. My sister-in-law was strong physically and emotionally. I am grateful for her companionship, strength, and care for my son. She passed away on my birthday at the age of 56.

The house was big enough so that we were able to rent out the basement apartment and that income paid for our mortgage. During the first year there, I had a great time updating and decorating it. For the first time since the age of ten, I was able to feel relaxed even though I was working two jobs.

During the first year in that house, my husband worked in the United States, traveling back and forth but earning no money at the end of this difficult year. Thanks to my brother and his kindness, my husband was provided with free room and board while working in the United States. He was also very attentive to my husband and me when we visited. My husband was very disappointed, discouraged, and therefore vulnerable during that time, which is why an acquaintance of an acquaintance was able to convince and manipulate him to invest in a furniture company. We invested $150,000 by taking out a mortgage on our home that had doubled in value. My husband put his heart and soul into that business, working seven days a week. Sadly, we lost all our money as the business went bankrupt since the other investor cheated us. According to people in the community, the con artist actually built a mattress that was filled up with money stolen from my husband.

This experience always reminds me of what my mother said about animals being loyal and only wanting love from us and nothing else. This man whom my husband trusted not only took advantage of him but took away our future. Sadly, I tried to do something about it, but because I could not prove anything, all that money was lost. This was very reminiscent of what had happened to my father back in Portugal all those years ago when many abused him financially. I specifically recall when he was cheated by the man driving his truck.

I was and still am so grateful for my full-time job with Nortel and part-time employment with Air Portugal at that time because it kept us going. Unfortunately, my husband was unable to find any work. After stressful months of unemployment, he was convinced by others to go to British Columbia for a 'guaranteed well-paying job'. So, he moved to British Columbia with the money we had left to get him started. Once in British Columbia, no job was in view, and once again, our money was gone.

Months later, my husband returned home thin, malnourished, and completely demoralized. In the meantime, as he was in British Columbia, I was trying to make things work here. I sold our furniture in an attempt to make up the money to keep up with the mortgage payments. It wasn't enough, so in a state of panic, I sold our home. It was a big mistake because I couldn't get a mortgage from the bank to buy another house, and so we were homeless. It was around that time that I left my husband. Now I was truly alone. Thankfully the only family I knew took us in, even though they had five children. God bless them because, without them, I don't know what would have happened to us; we would have been on the streets or in a shelter if we were lucky enough to get in.

While living with them, I was able to save up for my first and last months' rent. I found a home for my son and me right in front of the school that my son could attend. We lived in that house for two years while I worked two jobs. During that time, my son was badly hurt at school and suffered a concussion. One of my greatest regrets is that I feel I did not take care of my son as properly as I should have during and after his accident. It was not intentional, and I did the best I could. But looking back, I realize that he needed more from me. I did not provide him with the care and attention that he needed and deserved, especially since I was still working two jobs. I cashed in my RRSPs and my severance pay for the 12 years that I had worked for Nortel. To meet the minimum down payment required for the purchase of yet another house, I took on another job as a Portuguese interpreter translator, bought a little house, got borders, and continued working. My goal was, once again, to provide a comfortable home for my son and meet my obligation as a mother, all with the illusion that if I worked hard, everything would work out okay. So, I drove an old car that I shared with my son, and in order to give him the convenience of driving himself to school, I switched to the night shift. Life went on like this for about three years.

Around the third-year mark, I reconsidered reuniting with my husband because he was not doing well and was unable to take care of himself, which made me feel guilty and sad. Truthfully, I solidified that decision when I finally realized a life-long dream trip to Greece. It so happened that our plane escaped crashing after three emergency landings, and I promised God that if I was to see my son again, I would give my husband a new start.

I went into our relationship with no expectations, except with the expectation that I must do everything in my power to make things work. This renewed perspective carried me through many rough periods.

About a year later, I sold my home and bought a smaller home when my husband and I reunited. A while after we got together, I quit working for Air Portugal due to scheduling conflicts with my full-time job at Nortel. I, unfortunately, lost this job as well.

I had decided that I would give everything I had to make things work with my husband. I had always believed in hard work, and so I dedicated myself to making my husband happy and making our marriage successful. I threw myself into securing what I believed would be his happiness. As part of this newly determined self, I began to promote my husband as a singer, and I was even able to motivate him to record a CD. I was able to organize some very nice shows for him. He was a talented singer with a beautiful deep, romantic voice and very charming, so people were naturally attracted to him. I was actually enjoying putting this event together from various contacts acquired through volunteer positions, facilitating the sale of tickets and Portuguese media exposure.

Remember, dear reader, I spent my life feeling that I owed him for marrying me; I felt the need to make it up to him and the duty to make him happy, whatever it took. I thought I was helping my husband fulfill his dream of being a singer, even though he didn't ask me to, but after a while, I realized that I was wrong. Underneath this 6'2" attractive man, apparently equipped with all the right qualities to succeed, was a very insecure, broken man who, unconsciously, would sabotage opportunities because of his very poor self-image.

The realization that while my intentions were honorable, my actions were not his will nor his dream but my false assumptions of what I thought he wanted. This realization was part of my awakening. I wish I could have realized this sooner so that I could have spared him discomfort. Although I learned that lesson too late to benefit my husband, I keep it in mind daily so that I do not repeat my original mistake. One of the few highlights from my past was my heartfelt contribution to ***Amigas***. I still feel good about it and owe myself much gratitude for making it happen, as it became imperative to my awakening spirit of self-gratitude. "Amigas" means women's friendship. Allow me to briefly explain this Portuguese tradition that is related to Easter but not religious on its own. It's always on a Thursday, counting four weeks before

Ash Wednesday.

My friend's mother took it upon herself to pioneer and honor this Portuguese tradition by celebrating with a few friends - a heart-warming lunch, polished off by the traditional must-have delicious "malacadas" (Portuguese sweet fritters). I was delighted to be included! During the course of the meal when my friend, her mother, and I turned to each other with open eyes, knowing exactly each other's thinking and simultaneously bursting out the idea of taking it to a bigger venue to accommodate more friends. It was a thrilling moment! Amigas was an immediate success, and after a few years, we became the most popular event in the Portuguese community, selling out months before the celebration.

Why did it garner so much success?

This yearly event offered women the opportunity to get together to celebrate friendship. No men or children were allowed, just women enjoying a meal in each other's company followed by a live variety show. For many women, this was their only opportunity to take an evening away from their duty of being a mother and/or a wife.

For a couple of women who lived in controlling relationships, we were the only event they were allowed to attend on their own. That disclosure, in confidence, fueled all the work I put into the event and made it seem effortless. These husbands let them go because of the good image we portrayed in the Portuguese community and the connection of our popularity with the media and fundraising. These events were also a venue for women to showcase their talents, whether as a hobby or promoting the start of a small business.

Due to our popularity, a few talented women approached us, sharing that they were willing to share their talents with us. As a gesture of appreciation and affirmation for their participation, I provided financial compensation to the participants, feeling it was important to actively support their future endeavors.

The Toronto Star published an article entitled, "***Friendship Served in Large Portions,***" which featured the Amigas celebration. In addition, I submitted a yearly article to all publishing media, including the Portuguese newspapers, magazines, radio, and TV interviews on the event, including our fundraising efforts for hospitals, shelters, and the Canadian Cancer Society. Our event became so popular that men became intrigued and wanted to attend it, but we held firm and did not allow men to participate. Their only presence was felt when they served us the meal and were a part of the entertainment.

The raised funds from the second year of our event were donated to the only agency whose main purpose and focus was to assist and support Portuguese women who were victims of domestic violence.

A job offer for the position of employment coordinator was presented to me as a consequence of ***Amigas'*** donation to this agency. This gave me a wider window of compassion toward the unemployed. I loved that I was empowering those who were unemployed by helping them find employment.

I was and am so grateful that my new employment offered me excellent remunerations and a healthy benefits package because this was not only gratifying but also a life changer.

Amigas ended up being widely celebrated and anticipated by many. Unable to accommodate this event's demand, which lasted for 10 years, I appealed to other women to implement it in their own cities. As a result, ***Amigas*** branched out, stemming in cities across Ontario, Portugal, Massachusetts, the U.S.A., and anywhere else that the Portuguese language is spoken across the world.

Amigas was a gift; an opportunity to contribute. A chance to nourish an existing simple tradition to bloom into a bigger tree of opportunity that provided shades of comfort in women's lives. This came into existence by the three of us who had the enriching experience of making it happen. Our founder, my friend's mother, passed away at 104. I had the joy of organizing a commemorative

Amigas reunion on her 100th birthday. I've even had the pleasure of creating a website so that we could document and keep the spirit of *Amigas* alive all year long. For those interested, you can visit amigaspioneiras.com.

It was around this time that my ever-constant dream of building my own house resurfaced. After being together for six years and my husband working for that time, we bought an acre of land in Celadon. In order to buy the land and start building my dream house, we sold the house we were living in and moved in with my husband's cousin, who was gracious enough to provide a roof over our heads as a gesture of supporting my dream. My husband joyfully embraced this project while keeping his full-time job and working on the house after work and on weekends. I believe this was very significant for him as it increased his self-esteem. We happily moved into our new home in 2001, and in 2005 he had a stroke. As a result, he had to go on work disability until the day when he passed away. I am thankful that he was at a job that provided good benefits. To add to his illness and dependency, he also lost his driver's license, taking away that freedom.

Thankfully I was able to care for him. Then in 2013, he was diagnosed with stage two lung cancer. He was a fighter because he survived until 2020. One of the most amazing things was seeing how my son took care of his father. Even though the two had not gotten along well, my son was gentle and patient with his father and attended to his every need. Life is interesting. In 2015, my son had a terrible car accident, which left him with many problems, but the accident provided him the chance to dedicate himself full-time to the care of his father. I truly believe their time together was healing for both of them. Witnessing their healing contributed to my healing as well. I would soon join the two of them at home because, in 2011, I was diagnosed with Parkinson's. At first, I continued to work, partly because I loved my job and partly because I was stubborn and could not accept that I had to stop working. After a lifetime of constant work and struggle, I finally had to succumb and go on disability in November of 2012.

Again, I am in awe of life and the events that take place. Since I was on disability, it meant that I was at home and able to be with my son and my husband. I had been forced to stop because of Parkinson's, and it was because of Parkinson's that I was home full-time with my family. For the first time in our relationship, we felt like a family bound by love, pain, and uncertainty, yet grateful for the gifts we were able to experience together.

I began life as a child of two very kind-hearted and generous parents. I feel that my parents' generosity served me well throughout my life. I believe that it was because of their example that I had the strength to forgive my husband and reunite with him. That one decision, a decision of forgiveness, led to us finally being a family. Even though the three of us were ill, I feel that our hearts were healing. I have learned that everything is not always as it first appears.

Although he never said anything, I feel that my husband built that house as a way of appreciation and apology. I still live in it today, and although I know I will have to face moving as my illness gets the better of me, for now, I will stay and enjoy the home he built for me.

I am grateful that I had a second chance with my husband because I now realize that he, too, had suffered much in his life. His childhood was fraught with abuse and that experience lived with him forever. Even today, I remember his pain. I realize that he also carried post-war trauma from his four-year mission in Africa. Only recently, before passing away, he disclosed to a friend that he carried the body of his best friend in the African jungle for two days so that his friend could be sent back home to his family.

I will always feel and hear the pain and sadness in my husband's voice over losing his beautiful black childhood dog – Eulisses, with his shiny black fur, was his loyal companion. The emotion in his voice was as strong and painful 40 years later as it would have been when he witnessed his uncle drowning his beloved dog by throwing it into the sea. I now better understand the significance of that dog in his life - true love, an unconditional, irreplaceable friend; the kind of love that lasts a lifetime, just like what I feel for Leopardo.

At 15, he went to work on another island. Due to limited income, he was unable to come home for frequent visits. He remained there until he was recruited to the army at the age of 20.

As I reach the closing of this book, a new revelation raised up from my subconscious, but due to the gravity of the content, my first reaction was to push it back, to ignore it. Since it continuously kept knocking at the door of my consciousness, I finally understood that revealing the event holds the potential to help not only me but also all my readers since the purpose of writing this book is the desire to help someone under similar circumstances. By connecting the dots, the enigma of my husband's personality became a bittersweet reality through no fault of his own.

During my marriage of 44 years, my husband once told me that as he walked into his house, he saw a knife stuck in his mother's arm, covered in blood. He physically confronted his father but added nothing else after that. This could only have been in his teenage years since he left for the army at age 20. I responded with silence – the only way I knew – and suppressed this revelation once again based on the inability to deal with it.

Despite everything he saw and experienced, my husband had a 'heart of gold.' In spite of whatever his father had done, my husband had a great power of forgiveness. He never said negative things about his father, and when his father chose to be away from his family during the last ten years of his life, my husband chose to go looking for him, always saying, "Whatever he has done, he is still my father."

Despite the angst and upheaval in my life, I now find myself in a serene space, able to evaluate and give substance to the otherwise dysfunctional skeleton my husband lived in.

Though it takes two to tango, I now realize that disclosure on both sides is paramount in sorting out our differences while realizing the need to reconcile those differences without losing each other's identity. My space is now filled with comprehension as to my husband's behavior from early onset to embrace an adult life while being robbed of his childhood. My husband's lack of self-confidence, and lack of satisfaction with life, resulted in unrealized potential. With the exception of his labor of love, the building of our home that I presently live in bathed in bittersweet memories.

I am just sorrowful that this awakening only took place at the end of his life. I could not give him what I, myself, didn't have. My compassion for his state won me over to the point of protection. I sensed his internal peace when he finally filled the void of the father-son relationship, as my son so tenderly attended to his needs.

My intent is to give a voice to anyone who is going through a difficult time. Even though your challenges may be different than mine, we are joined by a need to heal and understand ourselves and our lives. To those struggling with the marital relationship, I encourage you to keep a diary of the worst episodes in your life so that you can balance them into a healthy approach to renewing your marriage.

Please, reach out for help to confront your false sense of normality and, in the process, bring about a healthier marriage. My husband's detrimental situation is that he never verbally expressed himself; reaching out for help would have put his life in perspective. Oh, I so empathize with his torment now that I find myself in a place of discernment! I will always feel and hear the pain and sadness in his voice.

By telling you my story, I aspire to relay how meaningless my life seemed to be, yet attaining victory at the realization that his life cried out for someone to rescue him, even though silence was his comfort zone. He too had suffered much in his life, mirroring my state of being. His childhood was fraught with abuse compounded by post-war trauma, which experiences lived with him forever.

Approximately one year before my husband passed away, I made the decision to bring clarity to my darkest secret that I believed he had a right to know – sex abuse. I was not sure how much he knew, and I was always embarrassed to talk about it. We both avoided going to deep painful places. I arranged for a couple of people whom I thought would be the right ones to provide support for both of us. However, I was wrong. He completely reacted in a manner that I did not anticipate - anger, denial, questioning my credibility of those horrendous disclosures. I was confused by his reaction, so I researched this topic. I can now justify his reaction.

The article was on "Cognitive Dissonance", and I immediately grasped its meaning and applied it to our situation.

It said, *"Sometimes, people hold a core belief that is very strong. When they are presented with evidence that works against that belief, the new evidence cannot be accepted. It creates a feeling that is extremely uncomfortable. And because it's so important to protect the core belief, they will rationalize, ignore, and even deny anything that does not fit in with that core belief."*

At this point in my life, I get to enjoy many things. Mostly I just enjoy life as it is. I appreciate everything that has happened and have applied it to my personal growth. There are moments when I can't believe that I can actually acknowledge all the terrible things that have happened to me, but that is what happens when you refuse to give up on yourself and on life. Just because you experience something traumatic doesn't mean that you can't recover. Recovery might take time, effort, and even pain, but it is possible and it is liberating.

I've traveled a long road to get to my liberation. Do you know that at one point, I was in therapy, and I never mentioned being raped? How could I? At that time, I still felt that by mentioning my assault, I was admitting to my weakness as I failed to prevent it. Sadly, until recently, the law in Portugal stipulated that a person could not claim rape due to the fact that he could fight off his attacker.

Imagine this, "a case of two men who had sex with a woman while she was unconscious" was judged by Portuguese courts as not constituting rape since there was no violence. Instead, it was regarded as a mere episode in an ambiance of 'mutual seduction'. Consequently, activists were demanding that Portuguese laws should define rape in a clear manner to focus on the lack of consent to determine if the case constitutes or not the crime of rape.[1]

It makes me extremely sad to think that women who are raped have to fight for their right to acknowledge that act of violence. I believe the law has since been recently amended.

I grew up with the notion that anything related to sex was not to be brought up either at home or at school. Consequently, that ignorance exposed me to detrimental sex-related situations and disabled me from fending for myself.

Sex was such a taboo that I think many people feared it. I know that for me, sex has been a curse because I have associated it with pain and violence all my life.

I cannot begin to understand the human psyche. I will never be able to fully understand it all because of my mere human condition. What I don't understand, I comfortably and trustingly leave it in the hands of God, the Creator of humanity.

If you look up the definition of rape, you will find numerous definitions; the main point is that it is non-consensual. I do want to stress that this chapter is about realizations, revelations, and awakenings.

In 2010, after my hysterectomy and the unconditional love of Leopardo, I took back control over my sexuality. One day it suddenly dawned on me that I had a choice. I might not have had a choice when that dirty old man picked me up and molested me. I might not have had a choice when I was fired because I would not have sex with my boss. I might not have had a choice when I was raped; all those events were violent, and I was overpowered. I now have the power to say no. It is the most liberating moment of my life. My body and I belong to me. I don't have to do anything I don't want to. I am liberated! Even with my illness, I am liberated. My life and my body belong to me. My decisions belong to me. What I do or do not do belongs to me. I have the power of choice. It has been a conscious choice to write my book and share with others my life experiences so that, hopefully, others who have been victims can find their own way to freedom. I want to encourage you to share your truth if you're able to and set yourself free. Find your source of inspiration and liberation.

My few good friends have also been a great source of inspiration and support. I always say that my mother asked God to send me Leopardo and that Leopardo's unconditional love sent me friends that I can count on. These good few friends have really helped me along my journey of forgiveness and healing. I am grateful for their love and support. They are a gift from God when I most needed one. I sense they have chosen me, as I have chosen them. These wonderful friends have made a great contribution to my life, and now I consider them part of it, added by the comfort that they're here to stay in this mortal learning adventure and for the next eternal existence. I feel that the pain associated with my family in Portugal has been replaced with joy.

One of my strengths is taking action. Inspired by meeting a woman who had written a book, I then contacted three friends from Amigas and suggested we start a 'book writing club'. During one of our meetings, I shared a bit of my life story and asked if they thought it was a book-worthy project. They all immediately encouraged me and said it was a great idea. With their coaxing and friendship, I decided to write "The Miracle Cat'. I am grateful for all of their support. For me, as you well know by now, my inspiration and liberation resulted from the unconditional love of Leopardo. I believe that Leopardo was heavenly sent to melt my stone heart so that I could finally feel the past and heal in the present. Love can really move mountains. Love really does have the power to heal. Love enabled me to realize that I could let go of pain, guilt, and fear and be free. Be free and live free. I now live free from the pain of trauma. I am free of guilt because I know and understand that rape, molestation, and even workplace sexual misconduct are acts of persons seeking to control others in unhealthy ways. I am free of my past trauma because I have the capability to now choose how I live my life. I choose. I decide. I forgive. I, Ceuzinha, am victorious!

EPILOG
Forgiveness and Gratitude

Forgiveness – it's a big deal! People write about it, lecture about it, and do workshops on it. Ever since Leopardo came into my life and I've been facing the experiences and memories of my past, I have also been on a voyage toward forgiveness of myself and others. It has not been easy.

The hardest thing for me to do has been to forgive myself. Feeling that I somehow allowed everything to happen has made forgiving myself difficult. Because I believe in God through faith in Jesus Christ, I am able to forgive myself and others.

Forgiving myself has meant letting go of the anger, frustration, and guilt I felt throughout my life.

Guilt is powerful. Guilt clouds your thinking. Even when I was being sexually molested, I took on the guilt. Those were actions of violence perpetrated by another party.

The general perception is that we need to forgive others first to facilitate forgiving ourselves, but I'm not certain that's always true. I know for myself that forgiveness has been hard work, deliberate work. Yes, you need to forgive others, but you also need to forgive yourself, and perhaps forgiving yourself is the first and most important step in your journey toward forgiveness.

I am happy to say that I feel lighter now that I have been able to forgive the people in my past. There is a great feeling of freedom that comes from forgiveness. It's as though whatever happened finally loses its grip on your soul. You finally become free and can move beyond the experience.

One of the techniques I have learned along the path to forgiveness is writing letters of forgiveness. I will share a few of my letters with you for two reasons: one, for those who hurt me - I want them to know they are forgiven and two, - to share with you, dear reader, that forgiveness is personal. Even though I still do not comprehend why my life has been so fraught with abuse, I do know that it was Leopardo who facilitated and gave birth to my desire to move forward and forgive.

My letters are specific to me and not perfectly written, but they have helped me move on. I wrote my letters nearer to the beginning of my *forgiveness* journey, and because of this, they are not exactly as I'd write them today, but I want to share them as they are so that you can know learning to forgive is a process.

My process began in 2014 when I took the initiative to write my first letter of forgiveness for my older sister. Actually, it was a letter and a recording that I brought to Portugal and had hand-delivered. As a teenager, I had the natural expectation of being protected by my older siblings, and I felt that did not happen, but I am grateful that I have been able to come to terms with the power of forgiveness.

I'd like to encourage you to write forgiveness letters because they really do help you free yourself from the past.

I have had an adventurous life. I am grateful for my life and for all the experiences I have lived through because they have made me the person I am today. There are times when I can't believe this has been my life. I've even had experience on television and radio as a volunteer, promoting information about "Amigas" and talking about domestic violence. Somehow, in some way, violence has always been a part of my life. I now realize I was working toward my healing.

In an effort to continue to support animals after my death, it became my dream to share my story by writing this book so that the proceeds could go toward supporting animals. Finally, my dream is becoming a reality; I am very grateful to those who encouraged and supported me. I have learned that in life, our pains and joys are shared by others; we do not live alone. We are affected by others, and we affect others.

It has not been my intention to harm anyone in sharing my story. This is my truth. My perspective of the events in my life. It is for this reason that I have not used names, not even fake names. I couldn't stand the idea of someone's name being used in a derogatory way. I want everyone to know that I harbor no ill feelings. I have forgiven everyone and everything. May we all live in peace.

LETTERS

I, too, need to forgive myself.

To this day, I lament not being informed of the sale of my grandparents' land and thereby not being given a chance to purchase it.

My sister had the conscience to inflict such pain not only on me but also on my mother. In 1980, it so upset my mother to know that some land was sold to outsiders by my sister.

I want my mother's forgiveness for my lack of courage in not trying to stop the sale of her dear parents' estate.

In 1995, depressed, with a lack of appetite and startling thinness, she attempted to say that she did not want to live and bear witness to her land being registered under other people's names. Once again, I hope she forgives me for not offering assistance.

To my father, may God give him a deserved, Eternal- Rest, as he endured great suffering at the hands of unscrupulous people who abused his ingenuousness and goodness. Sadly, even at the end of his life, he was abused by his own children as he witnessed the disappearance of his lifetime labor of agriculture and cattle being unnecessarily sold off on account of the selfishness and greed of others.

Magnificent Mother!

Mother, I want to thank you for the love I felt as a child. The nice dresses that you made sure I had for Sunday masses. The lessons of charity that I have learned from you as a child. You would make me deliver bread to the widows in the village who wouldn't have anything to eat.

You taught me the value of equality and a strong lesson about animal loyalty. The latter was imprinted on my mind at the age of six at that moment when a kitten was born deformed in our yard, and you said to me, "Animals are more loyal, unlike people. They are loyal for life if you give them something to eat and a little bit of love."

As the years went by and I stepped into my teenage years, you had no time for me in your chaotic life; I felt neglected and abandoned.

Unbeknownst to you, you entrusted my well-being into the hands of a sibling who didn't care about me. That sibling's behavior gave way to severe consequences that snowballed into sexual harassment, molestation, and assault which then evolved into rape, devastating me for life.

Mother, I forgive you.

But you must forgive me too, Mother, for not helping you when you most needed me. You lost your properties due to a couple of your children's mismanagement. I realized how much you suffered now.

I forgive myself for the times that I didn't reach out to comfort you and protect you from the pain brought on to you and for not being there when you most needed me.

Dear Father

Thank you for the kindness and generosity of your character. You believed in the good of humanity and had so much trust in others. You had the drive to be successful in the various businesses that you had in your life.

I forgive your naïveté. I forgive you for allowing those with fewer scruples to take advantage of you, for your inability to see the bad in people. I forgive you for putting me under the care of a sibling, which led to great harm in my life. I forgive myself for not being there when you needed me during the long devastating struggle with Parkinson's, which led to your death.

I want to say that I love you.

Dear Bright Brother

Through my child's eyes, I thought you were a genius. As a child, I had a strong admiration for you.

You were ten years old, driving the car up and down the yard. It was so spectacular! Before we were blessed with having electricity, you were able to light up our Christmas tree and *presepio* (Nativity Scene) with a simple battery plug-in. You were so knowledgeable! There was a light that, thanks to you, was shining on baby Jesus and I would just sit there soaking it in with the divine beauty of it all. We were happy to open the door to neighbors and people in the village to see our beautiful Christmas scene. I recall you doing a toy for the *presepio*. You would make helicopters move and even make a car from an empty spool. I thought you were so amazing!

Then, when I woke up to the realities of my life, I simply remember the time when you and another sibling exposed me to pornography in Lagoa. On the day I was raped, the rapist said that you had locked the door from the outside, and you told him to entertain me the best way possible.

I will never know if his words were true. I hope for both our souls that the rapist was lying because the thought of that being the truth is just as painful as being raped. Whatever the truth is, know that I love you and that I choose to remember you like my bright brother. Know that today I forgive you.

God bless you and I hope we meet again in this life.

Dear Brave Brother

Brave brother! You stood up for father as a child. That is the sweetest memory that I thank you for.

I remember that as a little girl, I saw you (younger than me by two years) stand up to a man who was using and abusing Father's kindness. Our father refused to believe that there were dishonest human beings. He was very naive that way. I saw you take your position against this man with your firm yet squeaky voice, telling him off for taking advantage of our father's good heart. I want to thank you for giving me the opportunity to baptize one of your children and live with that joy!

I want to forgive you for forgetting that I existed when there was a chance to buy a parcel of the family land. You and the oldest two siblings had the opportunity to buy, but I was simply forgotten. I forgive you for that and hope that you realize what you have done and forgive yourself.

To My Sweet Younger Sister

I hope you are saved. I want to start by thanking you for giving me the honorable invitation to be your maid of honor at your wedding. Unfortunately, due to very sad circumstances, I couldn't fulfill it. I hope you have forgiven me. At this point, I am not sure since the distance and silence have taken over our relationship. The most important thing I wish for you, as I go through the journey of my life, is that you were saved from the suffering I went through before I immigrated to Canada. I know that by now, you're aware of the details given in this book.

Part of me wishes that you were not able to connect in understanding the pain and suffering that I faced and now reveal, meaning that you were spared from going through the horrible experiences that unfortunately crossed my life.

I want you to know how much I loved you and how much you meant to me. I left you with my gold baptismal necklace, which I considered my most valued possession.

I wish you well and hope you can forgive me for anything that may have caused our distance.

Unfortunately, we cannot change the past, but we can look to the future.

To You, Rapist

I forgive you for your cruel and obscene actions. As you approached me and pushed yourself on me, I ran to the door, and you said my brother had locked the door from the outside. After that, I don't recall anything else but waking up the next day with blood and feeling that my soul and body had been penetrated.

I forgive you and hope that the most horrible thing you did to me has not been repeated to anyone else. I hope you came to terms with your guilt and asked God for repentance.

Hopefully, your children and your grandchildren don't suffer the consequences of your actions by being abused the same way you have done to me.

Your actions are undoable.

I have suffered this all my life. I lived in denial for forty years, but I finally reached a point when everything I had suppressed came to the surface.

I finally faced the truth that you brutally raped me and drugged me, as I don't recall it happening. I hope you are regretful of your actions.

I forgive myself for whatever I did not do to have avoided it.

To My Husband

I want to thank you for the past forty years and every effort you made to let me know that you love me. Thank you for the effort of building our house, which I understand you did mainly to please me.

I forgive you for the memory you left me on my seventeenth birthday. I wanted to spend it with you because you were my boyfriend, but I only heard from you I was second best. I was deeply hurt and saddened.

I forgive you for not answering the many letters I sent to you. You were my only connection. I needed to believe someone cared for me.

I forgive you for ignoring my last letter to end our relationship. You dismissed it.

I forgive you for slapping me in the car.

I forgive you for abandoning me with no food during my pregnancy while you caroled with your friends.

I forgive you for taking the money from my hands to fund your drinking and smoking.

I forgive you for a miserable wedding night.

I forgive you for the business ventures that only led to losing what I had worked for!

I forgive you for instilling guilt into me for not being a virgin when you married me. At the same time, I forgive myself for taking on that guilt.

I forgive you for the unkind words you clearly said over the years about owing you for marrying me and bringing me to Canada.

I forgive you and forgive myself for all the misfortunes that crossed our path.

I forgive you.

I forgive myself.

In Gratitude to My Mother for Helping Me See What Animals Have Meant to My Mother

My mother's dedication to rescue and care for animals has been stated several times, but what I wish to bring to your attention, dear reader, is the realization of what all those animals did for her.

Mother had their company on sunny and cloudy days.

Mother had their loyalty assurance when very early in life, she experienced human betrayal.

Mother had their honesty when she encountered dishonesty.

Mother had their comfort when she was victimized.

Mother had their irreplaceable value when her own possessions were stripped away.

Mother had the affirmation of their precious presence during her last few years as she moved on to eternity.

Mother was surrounded by her animals as she passed away. They would not leave her side.

She loved them. They loved her.

What Do Animals Mean to Me in My Life?

For the very little that I do for them – a little bit of love and food - I get a lot in return. I get their guaranteed unconditional love transpiring into full acceptance of who I am, independent of how I look and feel on any particular day. They are a comfort in my life, feeling their caring presence 24/7 as my companions and irreplaceable friends.

Here's a sample of a typical day – habitually, I get up before the sun rises. Immediately, I am warmly greeted by my precious cats. First things first, while I am brewing my coffee, my attention goes immediately to feeding them. Meanwhile, with a tank full of love, I step out on my deck as the sun rises to meet other unexpected little visitors. Take birds, for example; bird food is always served in abundance for their disposal. Then, we have the squirrels coming by and I greet them by their color...good morning, grayish, black, gray. They're precious and I'm happy to feed them. The flapping of a butterfly approaches and beckons my eye to encounter the enchanted beauty of its colors and precise design – another perfection of our Creator!

Inspired by the parade of these precious creatures, I cozily sit on the sofa and sign away petitions on behalf of abused animals in an attempt to reach out to absent ones and make a difference. That's why it's impossible to understand and even harder to accept how human beings' mission is set to destroy this beautiful world.

I remember as a young girl being distressed by the sight of uncaring human beings throwing defenseless animals – cats and dogs - into the ocean and in the water well across from my house. I am so relieved and grateful for my mother's generosity and compassion toward dropped-off animals, most of whom were injured and starving. Today, I joyfully embrace and follow her example.

ONE LAST NOTE

Before I end this book, I want to relay and stress the point that it is not only what I can do for the animals but, most importantly, what they do and did for me. I have learned that if I'm going to make a difference, I need to act now, regardless of my circumstances, and I take this opportunity to encourage my reader to follow and act on whatever passion is in their heart. Before parting of the ways, there are three more things I want to share with you. I want to take this opportunity to announce my next project, "Pets for Parkinson's." Please look for my next book. I'd also love for you to connect with me on Facebook, Instagram, and my website. I look forward to reading your thoughts and hearing your stories.

There is also a children's book entitled *Leopardo, The Miracle Cat,* written by Lucia Bellafante and published by Light The Way Publishing. It is both Lucia's and my desire that parents and children will better communicate when something traumatic happens.

It's rewarding to know that the children's book *Leopardo, The Miracle Cat* is inspired by my story and this book. Thirdly, I've included a speech by Joaquin Phoenix because I feel that his words reflect my heart so clearly. Joaquin Phoenix has so beautifully and artfully said what I feel. I have not won an Oscar, but I have won the battle over trauma, and I am grateful and feel blessed. Please read his speech, and I hope you feel as inspired by his words as I am.

JOAQUIN PHOENIX'S OSCAR SPEECH — A SPEECH THAT EMBODIES MY FEELINGS

"I'm full of so much gratitude right now. And I do not feel elevated above any of my fellow nominees or anyone in this room because we share the same love; the love of film and this form of expression has given me the most extraordinary life; I don't know what I'd be without it. But I think that the greatest gift that it's given me and many of us in this room is the opportunity to use our voice for the voiceless. I've been thinking a lot about some of the distressing issues that we are facing collectively, and I think at times, we feel or we're made to feel that we champion different causes. But for me, I see commonality. I think whether we're talking about gender inequality, racism, queer rights or indigenous rights, or animal rights, we're talking about the fight against injustice, we're talking about the fight against the belief that one nation, one people, one race, one gender or one species has the right to dominate, control and use and exploit another with impunity.

I think that we've become very disconnected from the natural world, and for many of us, what we're guilty of is an egocentric view, the belief that we're the center of the universe. We go into the natural world and plunder it for resources. We feel entitled to artificially inseminate a cow, and when she gives birth, we steal her baby, even though her cries of anguish are unmistakable, and then we take her milk that's intended for her calf, and we put it in our coffee and our cereal. We fear the idea of personal change because we think that we have to sacrifice something, to give something up, but human beings at our best are so inventive and creative and ingenious, and I think that when we use love and compassion as our guiding principles, it can create, develop and implement systems of change that are beneficial to all sentient beings and to the environment. I've been a scoundrel all my life; I've been selfish; I've been cruel at times, hard to work with, and I'm grateful that so many of you in this room have given me a second chance, and I think that's when we're at our best.

When we support each other, not when we cancel each other out for past mistakes, but when we help each other to grow, when we educate each other, and when we guide each other toward redemption, that is the best of humanity. When he was 17, my brother wrote this lyric; he said, 'run to the rescue with love and peace will follow.'

Thank you. "

---

[1]https://info.amicus-curiae.net/europe/portugal-finally-expands-the-legal-definition-of-rape/

Manufactured by Amazon.ca
Bolton, ON

29730435R00059